Shining a Light on Grief

real women sharing

real stories of love & loss

VOLUME TWO

edited by

SUSAN LATAILLE

**Shining a Light on Grief : Real Women Sharing
Real Stories of Love & Loss, Volume Two**
Copyright © 2023 Susan Lataille

Produced and printed by Stillwater River Publications.
All rights reserved. Written and produced in the
United States of America. This book may not be reproduced
or sold in any form without the expressed, written
permission of the author(s) and publisher.

First Stillwater River Publications Edition

ISBN: 978-1-960505-26-2

Library of Congress Control Number: 2022910540

1 2 3 4 5 6 7 8 9 10
Edited by Susan Lataille.
Cover & interior book design by Matthew St. Jean.
Published by Stillwater River Publications,
Pawtucket, RI, USA.

Names: Lataille, Susan, editor.
Title: Shining a light on grief : real women sharing
real stories of love & loss. Volume two / edited by Susan Lataille.
Description: First Stillwater River Publications edition. |
Pawtucket, RI, USA : Stillwater RiverPublications, [2023]
Identifiers: ISBN: 978-1-960505-26-2 | LCCN: 2022910540
Subjects: LCSH: Grief--Literary collections. | Grief--Anecdotes. |
Loss (Psychology)--Literary collections. | Loss (Psychology)--Anecdotes. |
Women--Psychology--Literary collections. |
Women--Psychology--Anecdotes. LCGFT: Anecdotes.
Classification: LCC: BF575.G7 S45 2023 |
DDC: 155.937/02--dc23

*The views and opinions expressed
in this book are solely those of the authors
and do not necessarily reflect the views
and opinions of the publisher.*

For Carmen,
With love, light &
gratitude!

♡ Wendy

To my son Nathan Cottrell who lives in my heart forever!
Without you, this book series would not have been created.
Love you to the moon and back!

and to my son Neil Facham
(Chapter 4)

SHINING A LIGHT
ON GRIEF

Contents

Foreword

by Diane M. Caine

You are not reading these words by accident. You, or someone who cares deeply about you, picked up this book in the hope of helping to mend your broken heart.

As one of the authors in volume one of *Shining a Light on Grief*, I am acutely aware of the pain you are in, how lonely it can feel, and how frustrating it can be to learn to live your life forward without your loved one. Grieving is hard, it's messy, and there is no right or wrong way to learn to live with it. Yes, *learn to live with grief.*

Each and every author, including myself, said yes to sharing their story with the hope of bringing just one person some comfort. To help you understand what you are feeling or not feeling is *perfectly okay*. Grief is not a passing emotion; it is something that will come in waves. Some days it will feel like an unrelenting hurricane; others will feel like the eye of the storm, calm and easy.

Each woman in this book and book one has traveled and continues to travel their own grief journey. Writing their story to share with you is another step of their healing process. Our hope and prayer are that this will be the same for you as you read the stories.

I am deeply grateful that Susan chose to follow her intuition and took the leap to start this compilation series. Grief is a topic that is so vulnerable and something that is desperately needed to be seen, understood, and supported.

Finally, as you read and remember, tears may come. I urge you to let them flow, for tears are the most healing of waters.

With much love and a comforting hug,
—Diane M Caine, Author
Shining a Light on Grief, Volume One

Introduction

by Susan Lataille

As I embarked on my search for authors for volume two of this series, *Shining a Light on Grief*, I heard many heartbreaking as well as triumph stories. It still amazes me how others have been able to navigate their losses with such grace and resilience; and how much a human heart can endure when faced with the unconceivable.

The book series *Shining a Light on Grief* started with a vision of women sharing their inspiration and hope-filled stories of love and loss. I could see how these stories could impact the lives of others by being able to identify with the authors. My goal is the offer hope and inspiration to those who are grieving.

Before publishing these books, I avoided my life's purpose for many years until I was finally ready to begin helping others, knowing this would also help me along my journey. My first step was to become a certified master grief coach. It was time! I had done research several times and found one that was best suited for me. I enrolled immediately after making this decision.

After becoming a certified master grief coach, I wondered what else I could do to assist others in their journey of grief. I'm someone who keeps all my options open and pays attention to what's coming into my awareness. I learned what others were doing with compilation books. It allowed authors to be able to share their experiences without having to write an entire book which certainly can be an overwhelming task, to say the least.

I loved this idea of being able to bring others' stories to light. The decision was made. I knew it was right because it both scared me and excited me at the same time.

First, I created a list of all the women I knew that had a great story to share that aligned with my vision. I reached out to each one asking if they were open to the idea and then followed up with a conversation. It was amazing to me that ten out of the thirteen that I spoke to said "YES." These were women who knew me, trusted I would deliver, and could see my vision. Our timeline was set, and off we went!

It was extremely rewarding and healing to work with each of the authors in both books. It was a journey that all the authors went through together with support and compassion. We met regularly for training and discussion. We all became very close. These women are like family to me.

Along the way, we discovered that through our writing, we continued to process layers of grief. It was healing in so many ways. I learned the true value of storytelling. I believe that everyone has an important story to tell. Throughout our lives, we go through different kinds of grief, from the loss of boyfriends or divorce, to jobs, to loved ones. Each experience that we have makes us the person we are today.

Through my own grief, I realized that everyone's story is unique, from the way the person died—whether through illness, suicide, or accident—to their relationship with their loved one and the way that they processed their grief. There can be many similarities in our beliefs, even though our way of processing our emotions and our broken heart depends on what we have experienced in the past. With each experience, we build the contents of our tool box with the best way for us to process our emotions.

Grief is still such a taboo subject that the name, *Shining a Light on Grief* came from the desire to bring a dark subject out of the shadows and into the light. I wanted to give people permission to share their stories of love and loss.

May this book be a great source of hope and inspiration. May you be kind to yourself by giving yourself grace and honoring your unique way of processing. May you see the possibilities in your life where you have moments of happiness in between your grief. Remember, you do deserve to be happy and "live" your life.

My advice to you, dear reader, is to take this book slow and have a box of tissues nearby. Each chapter touches the heart, body, and soul.

In love & gratitude,
—Susan Lataille

ABOUT THE AUTHORS

Melissa Coyle

Escaping the Darkness

My story is about a sister who goes to great lengths to save her brother from himself. Unfortunately, his addiction spirals out of control, and he overdoses, leaving behind a broken family and a sister who struggles to overcome the darkness that becomes her life. At the start of her journey, she learns that she is alone; her family cannot be the source of support she needs. Her unrelenting grief and stress lead to physical conditions requiring treatment and hospitalization. As her journey progresses, she learns that support can come in many alternatives and sometimes even surprising ways. As she mends the pieces of her broken heart, she learns that life, even a fulfilling and loving one, is possible after a tragedy.

I decided to share my story as I never want anyone to suffer the pain of loss alone. Many people do not understand grief and the incredible impact it can have on us mentally, physically, emotionally, and spiritually. I know that I, a trained psychotherapist, did not anticipate the roller coaster of emotions that shook me to my core after my brother died. I am sorry for your loss, but so glad you found this book. May it provide you comfort and strength when you need it the most.

Melissa Coyle is a Licensed Clinical Social Worker (LCSW-R) in private practice and has worked in behavioral health for over twenty years.

She works with adults on a multitude of issues, including anxiety, depression, trauma, coping skills, grief, and loss. She has a special place in her heart for grief and pet loss survivors and enjoys helping them transition from a journey of loss and pain to one of hope and growth.

In addition to being a psychotherapist, Melissa is a Certified Clinical Trauma Professional, Certified Grief and Loss Specialist, Certified Pet Loss Specialist, and a Certified Telemental Health Provider. She has worked with several animal rescues, is a member of the Association for Pet Loss and Bereavement (APLB), and is an active member of the charitable organization *"100 Women of Huntington."*

Throughout her work as a therapist, she has come to learn that there is a strong correlation between the mind and body. When appropriate, she offers alternative treatment modalities. She is Certified in Reiki, EFT/ Tapping, and Mindfulness. She also attended several series of classes on Spiritual Intuition, Chakras, Crystals, Seraphim Angels, and Sound Therapy, and is a Certified Angel Guide.

Melissa lives in Long Island, New York, with her husband Mike and three rescue dogs—Peanut, Bo, and Max.

Connect with Melissa:
Email: mcoyle.lcsw@gmail.com / petlosstherapistny@gmail.com
Websites: www.melissacoylelcsw.com / www.petlosstherapistny.com
Instagram: @grief_and_loss_therapist / @petlosstherapist

Patti Avin

When I Need a Friend, It's Your Name I Call

My story is about a unique sister connection. What one sister goes through during the last five years of her sister's life. I started writing this story only a few months after my sister's death. I hoped it would help me in the grieving process. I also wanted to share this story hoping to help others who have lost loved ones so close to them and who they relied on so much for their love and guidance. The loss of my sister is so deep it's like losing a part of myself.

Patti Avin is retired and has lived in San Antonio, Florida, since 2020. She is originally from Queens, New York. She lived in Levittown, New York for almost thirty years, then she lived for thirteen years in West Warwick, Rhode Island, near her children. Patti has been married to her childhood sweetheart, Michael, for 51 years. They have two wonderful children who they are immensely proud of and four terrific grandchildren who can do no wrong!

Patti left college after three semesters to go to work and earn money, so she and Michael could get married. She had many odd jobs over the years and eventually settled into administrative work for a health insurance company. Patti worked her way up to a Director position and retired from health insurance in 2009. She then bought a small tutoring franchise and enjoyed helping students reach their potential.

Patti enjoys bowling and reading. She belongs to a book club and is involved in her community. She enjoys cooking and trying new recipes out with her husband. What gives Patti the most joy is spending time with her children and grandchildren.

Connect with Patti:
Email: avinpatti@yahoo.com

Gina Lambert

Resilient Heart

For years I have been wanting to write my grief story. Suicide, cancer, drug addiction, divorce; each one of them devastating on its own. My story encompasses all of these heartbreaks over a four-year period. The road has been long and very difficult. Being the "fixer" in my family, I didn't take the time to process my own emotions through my losses. Although I felt I was dealing with the grief, I was actually pushing it aside and taking care of everyone else as a way to avoid my feelings. I struggled with anxiety, sleepless nights, depression, and fear. But I am here to share that there is life after loss. I am here to bring hope to people who are walking through the darkest days of their lives. We can survive. We can find a measure of peace. We can find happiness and love after loss.

Gina Lambert is the mom to two grown boys who, through their resiliency, inspire her every day to live her dreams. She has been a public school teacher for over twenty years. She has worked with all grade levels teaching health, science, and special education. Gina is a lifelong learner. Looking to branch out in 2011, Gina expanded her horizons by becoming a certified health coach through the Institute for Integrative Nutrition. Her passion for health and wellness led her to become an affiliate with The Juice Plus Company twelve years ago. She coaches others to make healthy lifestyle changes, create healthy habits, and live their own passions. Gina's dream is to teach as many people as possible about the brain-gut connection, how this connection affects our mental health, and how to use whole food nutrition to heal the body and the mind.

Connect with Gina:
Email: ginamarielambert@gmail.com
Website: www.gina1.juiceplus.com
Instagram: @better.than.ever17
TikTok: @beautiful_soul0331

Wendy Nadherny Fachon

A Letter to My Son

Since my son's passing, I often communicate with his soul from inside my head, mind-to-mind. I confer with Neil about my various projects, and having sensed and accepted his input on writing his story, it seemed natural to confer with him about writing my story, which is deeply connected with his. My story takes the form of a letter written to him, and the narrative shares our spiritual connection. This approach helped me to tap into my feelings about how our life together, his cancer battle, and his death affected me. I took much time and care to reflect on our mother-son relationship, all we had experienced together, and the grief I have experienced since his parting.

The suppression of my deep heartache and bitter sorrow through the first year led to physical consequences. My grief became embedded in my muscle tissue and literally immobilized me. I had to seek help on multiple levels—physical, spiritual, and emotional—to move through the pain and to the other side of it. That stage of my grieving process required me to recognize, fully feel, accept, and embrace the emotions of loss, sadness, despair, and incompleteness. This piece of writing has helped me to process these thoughts, experiences, and underlying emotions in greater depth and move further along my path toward healing. This project has been transformational.

For the past ten years, Wendy Nadherny Fachon has been a regular contributor to *Natural Awakenings,* the popular "healthy living healthy planet" magazine. She has been researching and writing about alternative regenerative modalities, healing foods, stress management skills, and spiritual work. Neil's illness occurred in the middle of this. She stopped writing to care for him and returned to writing after he died. Her hopes in sharing *this* story are to assist others in managing their own physical, emotional, and spiritual needs and to show how writing can be integrated into grief therapy.

She has been a guest multiple times on *Childhood Cancer Talk Radio* to speak about DIPG Awareness, the Right to Try policy, and The Jester & Pharley Phund. She hosts her own podcast series, *Story Walking Radio Hour.* Beyond this, she invites readers to check out her children's book, *The Angel Heart,* a spiritual and emotional story about a flower, written to help young children and parents through sad times to rediscover the joy, love, light, and beauty of *life.*

Connect with Wendy:
Email: storywalkerwendy@gmail.com
Website: www.storywalking.com
unite.live channels: "Story Walking Radio Hour" / "Angel Messages"

Jenell Bianchini

Write Out of Grief

My story is about love. How I found it, how I shared it, how I lived it, and how I felt when I lost it. While the story is about me, there would be no story without him.

My husband, Adam, died in August 2020 after a month-long battle with the Covid-19 virus. We were together for 21 years and married for 19 of those precious years. We had been inseparable, entwined, and so close to God that I believe HE used us as an example to show this kind of love to others. When my husband died, half of me died with him.

Since I have been writing and journaling since I was ten years old, this gift has been a constant in my life. Writing has been like a trusted friend or counselor for me, bringing comfort and peace through each and every upheaval I have encountered. Writing this chapter has been quite an experience for me. One minute it was therapeutic; the next minute, it was churning up an avalanche of pain and sadness.

But … it also reminded me of how truly blessed I am to have had this kind of love.

I had excellent coaching and feedback from the women in this group as well as some trusted friends. I am grateful for the opportunity to add my story to this volume of *Shining a Light on Grief*. I consider this pure joy if my story resonates with even one person who is struggling with grief and loss.

Jenell Bianchini is a native Floridian and lives less than 45 minutes from her sons and their families. It's a great comfort to her to know they are near if she needs them. Her stepson lives in Chicago, and they catch up by phone in between his trips to visit. Her children and grandchildren are able to laugh with her and talk about Adam and how they remember him. It makes her happy to know they can cherish his memory out loud each time they gather together!

Connect with Jenell:
Email: jenellbianchini@hotmail.com

Mary-Kate O'Leary

God Only Gives You As Much As You Can Handle

Witnessing my own Mom being a "Warrior," my story begins with the loss of my little brother when I was ten years old and carries on through the years of multiple losses. Like others, I worked through grief and loss at my own pace, with many highs and lows. My story, "God Only Gives You as Much as You Can Handle," highlights ways to include children in your grief and trauma as well as many lessons learned along the way. Participating in writing this story has been very healing. The amount of loss in my life has been overwhelming, but with great support, I have made it to this point and want to help others through their grief process.

Mary-Kate O'Leary is an Executive Director of a nonprofit called A Wish Come True. They grant wishes and provide resources to families that have a child with a life-threatening illness living in RI and MA. Mary-Kate can relate to these Wish Families from a sibling perspective as she has experienced extensive loss and trauma throughout her lifetime.

Connect with Mary-Kate:
Email: mkoleary23@yahoo.com

Michelle Girasole

Our Playlist, Cut Short

Ours was a lifelong friendship that lasted 45 years, from little girls at the sandbox through the teenage years, college, marriage, and motherhood, until Kris died at age 48, forever leaving a gaping hole in my heart. This story is one about the joys of having a best friend to dance through life with until her 20-year battle with cancer took precious moments of our lives away. I've discovered that music can bring back the happiest times and bring the smile back to my face—or trigger fresh tears, depending on the day!

I wanted to share this story because it might help others who have lost a special friend and may be reeling from the range of emotions that strike every time the memories come. I hope that readers might identify with our story and find some peace and comfort in the connection that your special songs and memories keep alive when your loved one has passed on. Go ahead and make your playlist, long or short as it may be!

Michelle Girasole is an award-winning author, innovator, and entrepreneur. After a career providing marketing strategies and services to clients, she is now working on a mobile platform that enables tourism-based scavenger hunts and self-guided tours called "Fresh Maps." Her podcast, "Get F.R.E.S.H." promotes food and recreational experiences, highlighting special guests with joyful conversations.

Michelle is the co-author of the award-winning book, *The Sassy Ladies Toolkit for Startup Businesses,* and a graduate of the College of Business at the University of Rhode Island, where she received her BS in Marketing and her MBA. She resides in Wickford, RI, with her husband, Rich, and two college-aged children. She loves to cook, walk in the woods, photograph sunsets and sink into a chair on the beach with a good book!

Connect with Michelle:
Website: www.freshrebellion.com

Elizabeth Phinney

Blake's Story ~ From Grief to Gratitude

The first time I experienced death was when I was eleven. I can see the exact moment: my mom got home from work and opened the back door. I was standing in the doorway of the kitchen and said, "I've been trying to call you. Where were you?" She looked at me, and so sadly said, "Auntie Tootie died." She burst into tears—I had never seen my mother cry before.

After that, as I got older and into adulthood, the older family would die, which you expect. I did lose a friend in high school to a violent death which was very difficult to accept. My dad died seventeen years ago, but he was older and ailing, so death was almost a gift. Then in 2009, I lost my son. Parents are not supposed to outlive their children, but there I was living every parent's worst nightmare.

Blake's life story was not a happy one. I share it here because his life was so short and filled with anguish, disappointment, and sadness, and then he died. But, when he died, he was the happiest he had ever been. As you will read, when he was four years old, I took him away from his father and was only then allowed to see him every other week. This broke his heart. He lived with his broken heart until he met the love of his life in college. His life mission was fulfilled. It might have taken him until he was 75 years old to find his true love and trust love again, but it only took him until 21. His life was complete.

Since his death, he has been a frequent participant in my life. He is a great support for me and the mission I am fulfilling. Just last week, his father passed away. I know now that they are reunited and having a grand old time together in the hereafter. They both waited long enough to be together again.

Elizabeth Phinney is the author of the upcoming book, *Thrive to 95 and Beyond* and an expert at Fitness After Forty Five™.

Connect with Elizabeth:
Website: www.fitnessafterfortyfive.com

Kelly White

Life Turns on a Dime

When Susan asked me to share my story, she originally thought I would write about the loss of my Dad. But whenever I considered sharing that story, I felt myself being pulled in a different direction. I was being guided to share my walk with mental illness.

I realized as I mulled over sharing my Dad's loss with you that I had been learning how to live with grief for years prior to his passing. Grief entered my world the day I learned that Abigail, my youngest daughter, was suffering from a serious mental illness and planned to take her own life. Although, it took me years to realize that grief was on this walk with me.

Each of our walks with grief is solitary in the sense that no two paths are the same, but the emotions we encounter along the way are universal. This knowledge that there is no one way to process grief and that I am not alone brings me comfort. My hope in sharing our story is that it brings you some measure of comfort and leaves you feeling less alone.

Abigail and I have come to realize that we were chosen to walk this path; so that through our healing, we could help guide other mothers and daughters as they walk along theirs. This has led us to start a podcast called *The Mother Daughter Journey*, becoming licensed C.O.A.C.H. Principals Teaching Partners in conversations, an author, and soon-to-be public speakers.

Connect with Kelly:
Website: www.themotherdaughterjourney.com
Email: info@themotherdaughterjourney.com /
  kelly@themotherdaughterjourney.com

Chelsea Force

The Unspoken

This story is about the unspoken struggles of so many parents while building their families. It's about the intense highs and lows of pregnancy, losses, miscarriage, and stillbirth. It's also about rainbow babies, hope, and the journey of healing.

I decided to take part in this book for many reasons. It almost seemed that the universe was leading me to this project. While it was incredibly intimidating at first to openly share such vulnerable moments and thoughts, I have high hopes that it will serve a greater purpose in helping others in their grieving journey. I hope other parents can read this and know that they are not alone. In the meantime, it has been a surprisingly therapeutic experience for my husband and me to communicate about our losses in a way we have never been able to before.

My name is Chelsea Force; I am a proud mom of two (soon to be three). I am an empath with a fierce love of life and a passion for helping empower others. I am a woman entrepreneur and a life-long learner. By trade, I am a martial arts instructor at an innovative program that focuses on kids' confidence and leadership development. I also help adults regain their own confidence and feel their best through health and wellness. I am so grateful for this opportunity to have an impact and help others through their grief that silently affects so many. Thank you for reading, and feel free to reach out.

Connect with Chelsea:
Website: www.msha.ke/forcefit
Facebook: Chelsea Hebert Force
Instagram: @MommyForce

Shining a Light
on Grief

CHAPTER I

Escaping the Darkness

In loving memory of my brother, Bryan Patrick Coyle.
"Loved beyond words. Missed beyond measure."
November 17, 1983 – March 13, 2012

By Melissa Coyle

I remember it being dark when I heard the screaming coming from upstairs. At the time, I rented the basement apartment from my mother. I'd like to say that the walls were paper thin, but they weren't. Her scream was loud. I'm embarrassed to admit this, but I thought my brother was physically hurting her.

Bryan was addicted to drugs and would stop by the house from time to time to see my mother and for money. He wasn't ever violent or loud, and I never feared him until I last saw him on February 13, 2012. He showed up, unannounced as always, euphoric and elated. He came by to give my mother a Valentine's Day card and to share with us, my mother and I, the life-changing plan he was going to create that would stop him and countless others from abusing drugs. He was dressed in the same baggy charcoal sweatpants he always wore, an oversized gray hoody, and a navy blue skull cap. This had become his look since revealing his drug problem to us years before.

As he spoke, I kept leering at the guy he had brought with him. Something did not feel right. I turned my attention back to my brother, who was still pacing back and forth and moving his arms in grand gestures as he continued with his plan for sobriety, on his own terms, with his own rules. He went on to describe a grandiose support system that he hadn't yet named but promised it would be more glorious than the 12-step programs that came before his. And he didn't intend to take on this task alone. This was when he introduced the guy on the couch, "This is my sponsor, Ben. He knows how well I've been doing and wants to help me with my plan." It was awkward, to say the least.

My mother and I had learned not to question or critique my brother, as he would simply shut down and leave. All we ever wanted to do was see him, and if that meant we had to play by his rules, then so be it. To be honest, though, all I ever wanted to do was hug him tight and not let go. That would be out of the question. This was a guy who was so uncomfortable with affection that he would say hello to the family with fist bumps, even on Christmas Day.

I wasn't sure what to think about this guy my brother brought into my mother's home. My intuition was telling me something was wrong. I started feeling anxious in my stomach, and my shallow, quick breaths were making it worse. I felt anger and adrenaline start pumping through my veins. I was about to jump out of my skin, but then my wise mind took over, and I was able to suppress my true emotions. There was no way this guy was a sponsor. I took a chance and asked, "What do you do? I've heard sponsors work hard to rebuild their lives when they find sobriety." Without skipping a beat, he offered that he was a contractor. "Tough work," I said. "Dirty work," he responded. I kept pushing my luck, "Why are you here?" "Your brother is my ride." "Ride where?" I asked casually, trying not to sound like a cop. But I pushed my luck too far, and my brother interrupted us and answered for him, "I'm taking him to work." Bryan then proceeded to talk about how well his sobriety was going. I was speechless. Sobriety? I had never seen Bryan this bad, this out of control. He kept this side of his life closely protected. He had us well-trained. He would stop by when he felt like it, and we could not ask any questions. We walked on eggshells because we didn't want him to get mad and punish us by leaving. We were an attentive audience for him, and there were a set of unspoken rules we all had come to understand. Basically, don't ask him anything about his life, how he was doing, if he needed or wanted help, and definitely don't express love or concern. I like to believe there was a part of him that loved us and wanted to see us but needed to protect us from his alter ego and his extra-curricular activities. I believe he struggled with shame and embarrassment.

My first attempt to learn about his sponsor, Ben, was a failure. This is not a good situation, I thought to myself. My intuition was steeped in discomfort, and I quickly started adding up the risks and peculiarity of that moment. It was late at night, and Bryan and Ben came home high. It was just me and my mother in the house. I had left my cell phone in my apartment. My mother sat at the far end of the couch, and I sat on the other, just an arm's length away from Ben. As my brother rambled and his sponsor made himself comfortable on my mother's couch, I took note of his light tan, pristine Timberlands, thick gold chain, gold watch, and the woodsy smell of his cologne. Ben was no construction worker, and if he was, he definitely was not on his way to work. I expeditiously played out several scenarios in my head, all of them with negative, possibly traumatic, and unforgivable consequences. Bryan was a die-hard loyalist to his friends. He could never imagine a friend betraying him, even if it was for all the right reasons. I knew that as his sister, my confrontation or seemingly disloyal actions would be seen as a mortal sin to Bryan. As a psychiatric social worker, I was usually quite good in times of crisis, but in this crisis, with my brother, none of the blueprints in my head seemed to fit. And I knew I was alone here. My mother never gave up hope that Bryan would get clean, and she clung to all of his words and stories as if they were the gospel truth. I understood why. I wanted to believe my brother's stories too. My stomach was in knots—my heart, head, and intuition were telling me this was bad and something had to be done tonight by me. I needed to clear my head. I understood, thanks to my clinical training, that I would never develop a plan or solution while my nervous system was stressed and in fight or flight. I politely excused myself, "Sorry, bathroom," I mumbled as I walked past my brother, head down, tears in my eyes. He didn't seem suspicious or alarmed by my leaving the room. He had become increasingly paranoid as the months went on. But this time, he was occupied with raising my mother's hopes.

I recognized that my time in the bathroom would have to be short, or my absence would be questioned. I leaned against the vanity and took some deep breaths. I had to calm down. I quickly remembered the advice

I shared with my patient that had a panic attack in my office. Breathe in slowly, through the nose for a count of four. Hold it. Breathe out through the mouth, slowly, for the count of seven. Repeat four times.

I knew what I was going to do. First, I was going to take his truck keys. There was no way I was letting him drive in his condition. Second, it was time for a reality check. I didn't know this person, this wasn't my brother, this was the drugs. I couldn't anticipate what his response would be. He had shown restraint with me in the past, but that was with a clear mind. But I had no idea how this version of Bryan, rambling and pacing, would react to confrontation. Bryan was a strong guy, almost 6 feet tall, and worked out and played handball like it was his job. Someone was bound to get hurt, and I didn't care if it was me. If things got bad, I would yell to my mother to call 911 and hope she would find the strength and wherewithal to do it. There were two of them and one of me. I flushed the toilet and ran the water. On the way out, I leaned into the mirror to reassure myself and spoke softly, "He's going to die if I don't do this."

With a deep calming breath, I opened the door and entered the hall-way. The living room could easily be seen from the hallway, but there was nobody there. Where were my brother and my mother? "Bryan" I yelled as I ran out the front door to discover that his truck was gone. I wanted to vomit. My stomach hurt, and I was angry and scared at the same time. I ran back inside, repeating, "Bryan?" It was at this point that I found my mother crying in the kitchen. With fear and uncertainty in my heart, I asked, "Where is he? Where is Bryan?" And with tears streaming down her cheeks, she said, "He left. He had to drive his friend to work." My stomach dropped as if on a dreadful roller coaster. "He had to take his friend to work at 10 o'clock at night? How could you let him go? He was so high he wasn't making any sense. He could kill himself or, worse, someone else." I ran outside again and into my apartment, where I ransacked my purse, desperately searching for my phone. I called Bryan. No answer. I sent him a text, no answer. My brother lived with my dad, so I called him. No answer. I ran back upstairs. "Mom, did he say where he was going? Did you give him any money?" She didn't answer me, but instead, sobbing heavily, she handed me the Valentine's Day card. In it, he wrote that he loved her and that she should not blame herself for his problems. He promised her he was going to get better and make her proud again soon. With the card in my hands, I slid down the kitchen cabinets and onto the floor. What did this card mean? Did he really think mom wasn't proud of him? I started crying harder. My brother was a beautiful, kind soul. Who was that person I saw tonight? It certainly looked like him, but it wasn't him.

I pulled myself up from the floor. Crying, I hugged my mom and told her it would be ok. There was nothing else we could do to help him that night and to try to get some sleep. I returned to my apartment, cried some more, and finally fell asleep. Around 1:00 am, now February 14, 2012, my phone rang. I didn't want to answer it. Nothing good happens at one in the morning. I checked the caller ID and did not recognize the number. I was afraid to answer it, but I did. "Hello?" I asked. "It's me, Bryan. Please don't freak out, but I got pulled over. I'm not under arrest. I just need you to come pick me up. I'm going to put you on the phone with the officer. He's taken me to the new precinct, and I don't know how to get here. He's going to give you directions. Ok?"

"Yes, ok."

"Hello, this is Officer Smith. Is this Melissa?"

"Yes."

"And are you Bryan's sister?"

"Yes."

"Good. I'm going to need you to come pick up your brother because he can't drive his truck home tonight."

"Officer Smith, why did you pull my brother over tonight?"

"I pulled him over for swerving across the yellow lines. He explained to me that he was just prescribed Xanax and didn't realize it was going to make him this tired. He seems like a good kid, so I'm just going to let him go with a warning." He then proceeded to give me directions, and I asked to speak to my brother again.

"Bryan, why did you get pulled over?"

"I was smoking a cigarette and dropped it in my lap. I swerved when I tried to find it."

He lied to me. I knew in my heart that this was my last chance to save him, even though he would hate me for it. I asked my brother if I could speak to the officer again. He became very paranoid and demanded to know why so I lied. "I took sleeping pills tonight, and I can't drive. I'm going to ask him if it's ok for mom to come get you. I also want to make sure I have the directions correct. I missed the name of a street." There was silence followed by a rather annoyed "Fine, just get here soon. He's keeping me in the back of his car." I was tired of being the go-to person for my brother. It was always me he would reach out to when he needed something. I was working harder on his sobriety than he was. I felt it was time to do something drastic, so I told the officer the truth.

Officer, my brother just lied to me. I think there is something you should know. My brother doesn't have a prescription for Xanax and was high when I saw him earlier tonight. He signed himself out of rehab five days ago against medical advice. He's an addict and is high. He has a problem and needs help. Perhaps it would be best if you arrested him."

"You want me to arrest him?" Officer Smith sounded completely shocked. "He seems like a good kid, and there's no reason to fill out all that paperwork. Just come and pick him up." I'm not quite sure whom I was most annoyed with; my brother or the cop who was making this situation even more difficult than it had to be.

"I'm sorry, officer, but I can't come and get him. I took sleeping pills and shouldn't be driving. Call our mother."

I quickly ran upstairs and told my mom what had happened and that the cop was going to call. Seconds later, he did. I left her bedroom. I didn't want to hear what she had to say or influence her decision in any way. She was either going to pick him up, and Bryan would continue to live this way, or she was going to have him arrested and let the drug courts try to save him from himself. She staggered out of her bedroom and into the kitchen, looking as if she had seen a ghost. Very much to my surprise, my mother went against every being of her soul and told the officer to arrest him.

A lot of crying took place that night, as well as great regret and fear. What did we just do? Would he ever understand how hard that was for us? We knew he would be angry with us. We were disloyal. But I couldn't watch him kill himself anymore. Now I could say I did everything within my power to help him. I pleaded to him as a loving sister, called in favors for him as a hospital employee, and took him to several detox centers and rehabilitation, only to have him sign himself out. I even went so far as to tell him to pick a rehab anywhere in the world, and I would max out my credit cards to make it happen. Nothing worked. I honestly saw this as my last opportunity to save Bryan, and I took it. If my punishment was resentment, anger, guilt, and regret, I would gladly do time if it meant that my brother could beat this addiction and live. Perhaps the courts would have better luck by forcing him into drug treatment. This was the end of the line; I felt it deep inside.

The next day, Thursday, February 15, 2012, my brother was to be seen by the judge. My father was there with a combination of disbelief and anger on his face. Bryan had apparently used his one phone call to reach out to our father. My parents had been divorced several years by now and had only spoken briefly by phone regarding Bryan's drug use. Nothing ever came from their conversations except hurt feelings and pissed-off mutterings of blame. I was physically shaking as I approached my father. My father, much like my brother, had an intense allegiance to his friends. I imagine it was some kind of unspoken rule amongst addicts. My father, an alcoholic, would never "snitch" and appeared to take great pride in this. As I opened my mouth to explain that I did this to save Bryan's life, my father cut me off to ask, "Did you really do this? Did you seriously have your brother arrested? Did you really think you were helping him?" And as he shook his head, he leaned into my ear and whispered, infuriated, "Do me a favor and never do me a favor. I don't ever want your kind of help." Almost immediately, I felt shame and humiliation. I was a snitch, and my father and brother knew it. Never mind their forgiveness, I started wondering if I could ever forgive myself.

We all entered the courtroom. I had never been in a courtroom, so I wasn't sure if I would see my brother upon entering the room. And if I did, would he be handcuffed? Could I handle seeing that? I bit my lip, hard to try to hold back the tears. It didn't work. Now I could taste my salty tears as they rolled down my face and a hint of metal as blood slowly trailed from the cut on my lip. My mom and I sat together. As each case was called, I would hold my breath, expecting to hear my brother's name. And then it finally was. He was escorted through a white door to a table situated in front of the judge. He stood there, motionless, as his case information was read aloud. "Not guilty," I heard my brother say, and he was released on his own recognizance. A court date was made for his next appearance, and once again, Bryan was escorted back through the white door from which he came. He never once looked around the courtroom to see who was there.

Later that night, I received an angry phone call from my brother. I listened as he reprimanded me for betraying him. I listened as he educated me that I had accomplished nothing and that he could simply walk down the street and buy drugs. I listened as he said that if given a choice between jail time and rehab, he would choose jail time. I was devastated and hated myself for hurting Bryan. That was never my intention. I apologized copiously, pleading with him to try to understand things from my point of view. He calmed down and said, "You shouldn't have done it." I was completely dazed by what he said next. "I like doing drugs, and I'm not going to stop." It took me a few seconds to process what he said. I didn't like it, but he was a grown man, and what he was trying to tell me all along finally sunk in. You can't help someone who doesn't want to help themselves. "I get it," I said as I wiped my tears away with my sleeve. "I won't badger you about your drug use anymore after I say this last thing. I love you, and if and when you are ready to get help, call me, and I will help you. No questions asked." The guilt was palatable as I ended the phone call.

Bryan was not always like this. He was not always an addict. It all started when he was involved in a car accident late one night. Two sports cars were drag racing on a seemingly empty road due to the late hour. One of the cars lost control, hitting the second car, which in turn hit my brother. Bryan and his car were launched into a tree. His car was totaled. One car took off while the driver of the other car called the police. My brother suffered soft tissue damage and injuries to his knee, shoulder, and back. His treating physicians sent him to a pain management specialist who prescribed him increasing doses of oxycodone for his pain. This was at the beginning of the opioid crisis, and patients and the public were not properly informed of the addictive nature and dangers of this painkiller. At one point, my brother's pain management doctor was investigated, arrested, and found guilty of overprescribing the drug and selling scripts from the trunk of his car.

I had no shoes on when I ran upstairs that night. I heard the screaming. My God, I thought, what is going on in there? The main door was open, and it was just the storm door I had to step through. Before I stepped inside, I peered through the glass, expecting to see my brother, but I didn't. The screaming got louder as I opened the door and ran towards my mother. She was beyond hysterical. She could barely speak. She shoved her phone into my chest and said, "It's your father." My father? I thought. What could he have said to make her this upset? I pulled the phone away from my chest and up to my ear as I walked to the front door. "Dad?" I asked, confused. "What's going on? Why is mom so upset?" All I heard was silence coming from the other end, so I asked again, "Dad, it's Melissa. What the hell is going on?" And this time, he answered. "Bryan is gone." I knew what he said and what he meant, but I had to ask again because maybe I heard him wrong or hoped I had heard him wrong. "Your brother, Bryan. He's gone. He's dead." I fell to my knees, feeling nothing as they hit the ceramic tile floor, grasped my arms, and with my forehead pressed into the area rug, I howled, "No, No, No, Please God, No." I wanted to call him a liar. I wanted him to take back what he said. I put the phone back to my ear and asked for more information. "Where is he?" I asked, afraid but wanting to know the answer. "He's at home. The police and an ambulance are here," he said with no emotion. But I knew my father well enough to know that he was trying to remain stoic, and there was a lot of pain hidden behind his words. "Ok, so he overdosed. Are the EMTs still working on him?" I asked, praying to God my dad would give me a different answer this time. "No." He said, "He was dead when they got here." I still didn't believe him. Why would he say such cruel things? I asked if the police were still there. "Yes," he answered. "Put the officer on the phone," I demanded. "I want to speak to the officer in charge." I knew this was going to happen. He died exactly one month after I last saw him. It was March 13, 2012, a day I would never forget and forever hate. Clearly, I was not of sound mind and went into survival mode. I completely shut down and focused only on getting to my brother. I felt absolutely nothing. I stopped crying. I was just a talking head following some unknown script.

"Hello, ma'am, this is Officer Hines. How can I help you?"

"Where's my brother? What happened to my brother?"

"I'm sorry, ma'am, but your brother is deceased. We are waiting for crime scene detectives."

"Crime scene detectives? What the hell happened to my brother?"

"We believe your brother overdosed, but it is police procedure to treat it like a crime scene until we can confirm the cause of death."

"I can be there in forty minutes. Please don't move my brother's body until I get there."

"Get here as fast as you can, and I will see what I can do. I can't make any promises, ma'am, but I will try."

Now at peace, seemingly in control and momentarily content in the land of denial, I grabbed my mother by the shoulders and told her to get her purse and keys. "Why?" she asked through a face full of tears. "Because we are going to see Bryan, that's why. Meet me outside." I was going to find out what was happening. I was going to get the full story. I was going to fix this, just like every time before. Not a sound was heard in the car other than the voice from the GPS system. We couldn't remember how to get to my dad's house. That was the longest car ride of my life. "Turn left here," I shouted as I recognized the road he lived on. As we drove down the street, all I saw were lights and bright yellow crime scene tape tied around the house. It was like pulling up to a stomach-churning Law and Order episode. I opened the car door and ran to my father's front door. It was wide open, and there were uniformed people everywhere. I could see flashes from a camera presumably being used to document the scene. I couldn't see into Bryan's bedroom. I was quickly spotted and asked to take a few steps back. "No," I said, and I shook my head from side to side. "That's my brother in there, and I need to see him." The officer touched me on the arm and said, "You can't go in there right now. It's a crime scene. Let them finish with their pictures, and then you can go in." I turned around and walked to the front of the house. I saw my father just standing there in a daze. I hugged him and started crying again. This time I got to look my father in the eyes as I asked him once again, "What happened to Bryan?" My father picked his head up and met my eyes with his as he said, "He's dead. He overdosed. I found his body in his bedroom when I got home from work. I went in to ask him if he wanted some of the chicken I had brought home. I called the police and tried CPR, but he was so cold." And with that, his eyes filled with tears. You're so useless, I thought to myself and went to find someone that could give me better answers, answers I wanted to hear.

My anger and an overwhelming sense of helplessness took control of me as I was directed to the coroner, a Physician Assistant. "The county coroner is out on another call," he said as if I cared. I asked him what felt like a hundred questions: Where is Bryan? What room was he in? What position did you find him in? What was he wearing? What did he take? How did he die? Did he die quickly? Could he have been saved? And then came the medical questions. I was studying to become a physician's assistant at the time and was mid-way through anatomy and physiology. "Did he have a heart attack? Did his heart stop? Did he go into respiratory arrest? Did he choke? Did he gasp for air?" I needed to know everything. It was the only way I was going to accept that my brother was truly dead. That's when I spotted the crime scene team walking toward the front with their cameras. I could see Bryan now. They were done taking pictures, so I ran to the door, where I was met by the same officer as before. He wasn't letting me in, so I figured he must have forgotten what he said to me earlier, that I could go in after they finished processing the scene. I reminded him of what he had said. He turned to me, and in the most direct but softest tone, he said to me, "Trust me. You don't want to see your brother like this." I was taken aback by his comment. Why wouldn't I want to see my brother? This made no sense to me. I needed to see him with my own eyes. The coroner came walking towards me. He had put on surgical gloves and turned to me and repeated what the officer said, adding, "You don't want to remember him this way."

In front of the house, my mother and father stood on opposite sides of the lawn, each grieving in their own way. I hated them both. How could they let this happen? I didn't know what to do with myself, so I went and stood by my mother. The coroner called me over. We were now standing in the street. He told me it appeared that my brother had overdosed and most likely died from respiratory arrest in the early hours of the morning. He said he would know more once the autopsy was performed. "Autopsy? You said he overdosed. Can't you just do a blood panel to find out what he took?"

"No, it's the procedure to perform autopsies when someone dies at such a young age. Your brother was only twenty-eight, and we have to rule out any other possible causes of death."

I felt sick and dizzy. I had seen autopsies performed on TV, and the thought of someone cutting into my brother and removing his organs horrified me. The coroner started asking me personal questions: "How do you know so much about the body? Not many people know what questions to ask a coroner. So you're a social worker going back to school to become a Physician's Assistant? You're going to be able to help a lot of people with a background like that, especially if you choose to work with the coroner's office. Think of all the grieving families you could help." My head was whirling, and everything seemed to be moving in slow motion. I went temporarily deaf as I couldn't process any more disturbing conversation. I could see everyone's lips moving, but I heard nothing that came out of them. What was happening here? Why was he bothering me with all of these pointless questions? My brother's dead, and he's over here making small talk. And then it hit me. He was distracting me. I looked up, and to the right, I saw a gurney being carried away from the house. My brother, inside a white body bag, was being placed in the back of the ambulance. It was different from the movies I had seen, where bodies were usually zipped in black bags. This white bag was a surprise to me. I ran over to them, "Wait, wait, can I just see his hand? Please? Just his hand?" Their answer was an unsurprising "No." I took a few steps back and watched from a distance as they finished loading my brother into the ambulance and drove away. I watched the truck drive away until it became nothing but a blip in the distance.

I walked over to the giant oak tree on the edge of the property and used it to support myself as I scrolled through my phone. I was plagued by an intrusive thought that kept getting louder in my head. I found my therapist's number and called him. I don't know why, but I called him. Perhaps I needed to confess my sins to someone unrelated to me before the rest of the family figured out what I did. I was a hysterical mess by the time I made the phone call. I imagine most of what I said was unintelligible wailing. I was ugly-crying by now and hyperventilating when I told him, "My brother is dead, and I killed him. It's my fault." I repeated myself several times until the hyperventilation took over, and I could no longer speak. That's when Dr. Craig finally had a chance to speak. He calmed me down by reminding me to breathe and waited patiently as I took some deep breaths. When I regained some composure and was able to speak again, Dr. Craig asked me to explain what was happening. I don't recall the full conversation verbatim, but I told him what I had done, how I had killed my brother by having him arrested. "He killed himself by overdosing because I betrayed him and broke his heart." I needed someone or something to blame, so I blamed myself and the actions I took with the intention of never having to experience this exact inexplicable pain. I was experiencing overwhelming guilt and needed to confess what I believed to be my fault. Dr. Craig kept repeating that it wasn't my fault and that, unfortunately, overdoses happened every day. He was right. It wasn't my fault. I felt like I was going crazy. Why were my thoughts torturing me like this? In an odd sort of way, I think my brain was trying to protect me. This nightmare wasn't over yet, and it was easier to feel guilt and anger than the pain and sorrow of loss. Guilt is regret gone bad, and I had a lot of regret at that very moment.

I was still over by the oak tree when I heard the arguing. My mother was in my father's face yelling. "You killed my son!" There were still officers on the scene that broke it up. Everything after that is a blur. The next thing I remember is getting in the car to go home. I remember looking in the car mirror on the visor. My head was pounding, and my eyes were so puffy from crying that I could barely see through them. I stumbled out of the car and into my mom's house. My sister, Madison, met us there. She had driven from her home in Queens. I couldn't understand how she made the drive. I could barely walk. Madison and I sat on one couch, my mother on the other. The silence hurt my ears, so I broke it, "We have to call the family." The three of us split up the list of family members to call. This chore was the hardest for me. I had to tell family, whom I hadn't spoken to since 2006, that Bryan was dead. I did not like my mother's family. There were five siblings, and each of them treated my mother poorly. I was repulsed by all of their behaviors, and when my Nanny died in 2006, I called it quits with her dysfunctional family.

After all the calls were made, we returned to our seats in the living room, each of us sipping a glass of pinot noir. There wasn't much to say, just tears to shed and disbelief to work through. The next few days were tough, especially for me. I noticed that my mother and sister had an attitude toward me, and this attitude extended into my mother's family. It seemed like I couldn't do or say anything right. Everything I said or did seemed to enrage them. It didn't help that I grieved differently than my mother and sister. I needed to externalize things, to talk. They didn't want to talk about him. It wasn't until a few days later while discussing the limo pickups for the funeral, that I learned why they were really angry at me. I had mentioned my father, and my mother lost it and berated me, "How dare you bring up that man's name? He killed my son!" She was so angry, breathing between clenched teeth. I was bewildered and didn't know what to say. As it turns out, she wasn't the only one who felt that way. So did my sister. My mother and sister believed that my father killed my brother as he was an absentee father and a drinker. My mother made it very clear that my father was not welcome at Bryan's funeral. I tried reasoning with my mother. "You can't just not invite Bryan's father to the funeral. This is crazy." My sister added that she didn't want him there either. I tried so hard to reason with them both. I even spoke to everyone in my mother's family, and all of them acted like I was the one being unreasonable. One would hope that a tragedy like this would bring a family together. Unfortunately, this pulled us apart even further than we were already. I had absolutely no support, so I called the only other person I could think of, my dad's sister, Aunt Genie. Aunt Genie told me she couldn't help me. "Look at how they are treating my brother. Imagine what they would say or do to me." I couldn't believe it. "Aunt Genie, Bryan was your nephew. Your brother's son. You're not coming to the funeral? I need you. Dad needs you." "I'm sorry, kiddo, but I can't do it. I will send flowers. Do me a favor and keep taking care of my brother, ok?" I couldn't understand why this was being dumped on me. I didn't want to be the only one fighting for dad, but they left me no choice. In hindsight, I guess I could have just kept my mouth shut and let my dad fight his own battle, but it just seemed so very wrong to abandon him like that. Besides, that was the role I was most comfortable in, the family fixer. I carried the family cross and took responsibility for everyone else's problems in addition to my own.

Luckily I went to school with the oldest daughter of The Mabel Funeral

Home, and my sister went to school with the youngest daughter. Our families had known each other for years and walked us through everything that had to be decided. My mom was beside herself and delegated many of the decisions to me. Once again, I didn't want to be making the decisions. They were already upset with me, and I knew this would make things worse and be used against me at some point. I did it anyway, for my brother. I had always taken care of my brother, and this was just another way of caring for him. I chose the prayer cards, songs, prayers, and church readings, ordered the thank you cards and completed all the paperwork. I contacted the local newspaper and wrote the obituary. I chose the color and design of the headstone, including the saying it bore: "Loved beyond words, missed beyond measure." The funeral home helped us choose the flowers and casket because I just had nothing left to give. We decided on white roses and green carnations for the top of the casket. Bryan was proud of his Irish heritage, and he was to be interned on Saint Patrick's Day. I made the deposit for the funeral too. My mom hadn't thought ahead and forgot her checkbook. My mother paid me back, but it wasn't the money that obliterated the remaining pieces of my heart but rather the alienation when I needed family the most. I felt so alone and isolated. I was on the outside of the snow globe looking in.

I chose Bryan's burial outfit: a gold and white short-sleeved collared shirt, one of his nicest pairs of jeans, and his Yankees cap. It was the outfit he wore to my 30th birthday dinner. It remains one of my favorite pictures of him to date. He was so handsome, tall, fit, and blonde with ocean-blue eyes. It's the way I will always remember my brother.

The morning of the wake, I went to the jewelry store and purchased a white gold cross with a diamond accent. I refused to go to the wake without a new cross, a cross just for Bryan. I also wanted a black shawl. I wanted everything to be perfect for him. On the way home from the mall, I stopped at the local sports store and bought a jug of handballs. My brother loved handball and was good at it too. He had won medals and a trophy. He played so often that he had to use duct tape to keep the bottom of his sneakers together. I gave a handball to all of the immediate family members and asked them to write a message for Bryan on it and put it in the casket when they said their goodbyes. My sister's friends put together some beautiful picture boards, and I placed his Yankees cap and handball medals in the casket with Bryan. I also brought the family scrapbook to put on display. Bryan hated taking pictures as he got older, so the majority of pictures were of him as a younger man.

I felt invisible as several people walked up to me and offered condolences directed toward my mother: "I'm so sorry for your loss. Your mother must be devastated." "How is your mother holding up?" "I'm so sorry. Please tell your mother our thoughts are with her during her time of need." I began to wonder if I was in a Twilight Zone episode. I wanted to wave in their faces and say, "Hi, I'm here and hurting too. I just lost my brother." But no one seemed to identify with sibling loss. My pain and loss were overlooked. I was the oldest in a family of three. The three of us had snowball fights, made mud pies, and opened Christmas gifts together. Without being one of three, who was I? It felt like everything I remembered of my childhood belonged to somebody else. I began to think of all the times he would come to meet me as I got off the school bus. There was also the time we pretended to be radio DJs and recorded ourselves announcing songs and doing impressions. He was the kid in the classroom who would come home hungry because he would share his snacks with all of his friends. The guy with great love and talent for drawing and music. The young man I would hang out with and talk to in the garage when he had a smoke. My brother who rushed me to the doctor when no one else was around, and I was sick with a 102 fever. He made sure I was seen by the doctor, that my prescriptions were filled, and that I had a full bottle of Tylenol. I would never see my brother grow up, get married, or have a family.

The wake was heart-wrenching and distressing. My therapist came, and it was the first time I felt supported and safe throughout the entire nightmare. There was no eulogy as no one could find the words for such a travesty. My brother looked beautiful in the casket and so at peace. The kind of peace and stillness we all strive for but never quite seem to achieve in life. They shaved him. They dressed him. In that casket was the brother I had known prior to his addiction. I said my heartfelt goodbye, kissed him on the forehead, and placed my hands over his. I asked someone to take a picture of me kissing my brother for the very last time. I haven't looked at that picture since it was developed, but it brings me solace to know I have it.

The coffin was all set up and covered in green and white flowers. As we walked past the minister, he handed us a flower to toss on the grave as a final goodbye. My father and his friends stood on one side of the coffin, and my mother, her family, and her friends stood on the other. Madison lurked in the back, holding onto her friends, seemingly always on the verge of fainting. It was like watching gangs ready to attack at the slightest provocation. I crossed the lines of battle and displeased my mother and sister once again. I hugged my father and introduced myself to his friends.

The minister said some beautiful words and a closing prayer as we each placed our flowers atop the casket. It was hard to watch. It was hard to leave. This was the end of the road, quite literally. I watched as they slowly lowered my brother into the hole beneath him, realizing I would never see him again.

We hosted people back at my mother's house, and I quickly came to learn that people don't know what to say when someone dies. Actually, it was quite clear that it made them uncomfortable and awkward, which, in turn, made me uncomfortable. I hated all the empty, rehearsed sentiments I had gotten, like: "I feel your pain." "God called him home." "This will make you stronger." No, none of those things were true. No one could possibly understand what pain I was feeling. I didn't really care about what God wanted. I was angry at him for taking my brother. No, it didn't make me stronger. It made me feel helpless, weak, and broken. Nothing about this would make me feel stronger. It traumatized me. It made me wonder what the point of life was and whether it was worth such pain. It made me experience negative emotions I never knew I was capable of.

Strangely, the funeral was the easy part because there were many distractions and so many people around. Once the funeral is over, everyone disappears, leaving you alone with your ghosts and thoughts. I was scared at night. I swore I could feel his presence and, at times, see him. I thought I was slowly losing my mind. Grief is a beguiling emotion. At times I felt tremendous emotional and physical pain and wondered how I would ever survive. At other times the grief presented as utter emptiness and loneliness, like an endless black hole. And yet, at other times, it presented as unrelenting guilt, leading me to replay every single interaction we ever had, looking for what I had missed.

I became depressed. I didn't want to live in a world without my brother in it. I dreamed of the day I would wake up not drenched in sweat, mid-panic attack, gasping for air. Days became nights, nights rolled into days, and this vicious cycle went on and on. I gave up trying to sleep and took up coloring. It calmed my mind and my soul temporarily. On really bad nights, I would color with my non-dominant hand as it took extra focus and attention. I couldn't feel the pain when my brain was already occupied by another thought or feeling. Food had no taste, and I had no energy or desire to eat anyway. Buddy, my Chihuahua, and I would lay in bed all day, curled up and crying. The television was on, but I couldn't follow any of the storylines, so I began watching cartoons. It was background noise, and I would just stare at it for hours. It didn't matter what the characters did or said. They were colorful and easy to follow.

I couldn't think straight or make decisions. There was a thick fog attacking my cognitive skills. The migraines came daily, and the stomach pains were overwhelming. I had broken through the denial but was still quite angry. I started to engage in magical thinking, begging God to take me and let Bryan live. I was literally living in the dark with the shades always closed and lights out. I preferred candlelight or the soft glow of the television for light. For some unknown reason, I found comfort in the dark. Perhaps it was because the outside world now matched what my inside world felt like: darkness.

One day my body decided it couldn't take the stress anymore, and I began to experience unrelenting visceral pain and a burning sensation in the middle of my chest. My stomach would go in and out of spasm, making it difficult to walk at times. I went to see a gastroenterologist who had me undergo multiple invasive and unpleasant tests. I was diagnosed with Irritable Bowel Syndrome, or IBS, and Gastroesophageal Reflux Disease, or GERD. I was informed that acid had eroded some tissue in my esophagus. I was placed on an anti-spasmodic, a benzodiazepine, and a proton pump inhibitor and told to avoid stress whenever possible. Avoid stress? I laughed to myself. My world was one enormous, sweeping ball of stress. I was not surprised by the diagnosis. I knew that IBS was common in people dealing with trauma and anxiety. On three occasions, the medications were not enough, and I ended up in the emergency room for pain and symptom management via a morphine drip. On one occasion, my mother and her brother picked me up from the hospital. The other two times, I had to take a cab home as my mother "couldn't deal with me anymore."

Approximately one week after my last ER visit, I began to experience stomach pain and gastrointestinal distress while working at the hospital. A nurse took my vitals and paged the on-call doctor. I was admitted to a medical unit secondary to an IBS flare-up and dehydration. I called my mother and asked her to please bring me some clothes. She said yes but never showed up. It was embarrassing to admit to my co-workers and department director that my mother wasn't coming. They were so kind and went to the hospital gift shop and brought me some magazines to pass the time. I didn't deserve their kindness. I was a hard worker but was irritable and short with them at times. I was under tremendous pressure at home, and it was trickling into my work life. I was losing control, and it was getting harder and harder to keep it together. When I was discharged, I drove myself home.

To make matters worse, I was involved in a car accident on May 13, 2012, exactly two months to the day my brother died. It was mother's day, and I was driving on the Long Island Expressway when I was hit by a truck. My car went into a spin, ending up facing the wrong direction on the highway. I thought for sure I was going to die, and I didn't care. The next thing I remember was trying to get out of my car as I had been hit in the driver's side door. I had no idea where I was or what had happened. Someone called the police, and I declined an ambulance. I remember the officer saying he was shocked I was alive and that my car wasn't totaled. I believe Bryan saved my life that day.

The next day I started feeling pain everywhere in my body, and it felt like knives were being stuck into the back and top of my head. I couldn't stop going to the bathroom, and the visceral pain was more intense than I had ever felt. I could barely walk or speak. My lips were blue. I called 911 and was told I had briefly lost consciousness in the ambulance. I remember being worked on in the emergency room and couldn't understand what was happening. Apparently, I had a concussion and a severe C-diff infection and was in shock. I was so weak. I asked the doctor if I was dying, and all he said was, "You should call your family." I couldn't believe this was happening. My brother had just died, and there I was, fighting for my own life. Someone went through my bag and handed me my phone. I called my mother and told her I was in the ER. My mother and her friend showed up as they were preparing to move me from the ER to a private room with a bathroom. I got up several times to go to the bathroom. At one point, on my way to the bathroom, I remember having trouble breathing and falling back into the hospital bed. Alarms started going off, and I slipped into septic shock. They rushed me to the Intensive Care Unit, where I spent one week fighting for my life and my colon. There was talk of removing a piece of my colon to save my life. I begged them not to cut up my colon and had the hospital contact my primary gastroenterologist. Together they came up with a plan. They were going to push fluids and strong antibiotics for a few more hours and see if I responded. By the grace of God, I responded and continued to get stronger. I was eventually moved to a regular unit. "Thank you, Bryan," I said aloud as I contemplated how extremely lucky I had been again.

My mom barely visited, and when I asked her to come, she would make me beg and tell her how much I loved her. I'll never forget the night she left after only a short while, as it was "Swedish meatball night" at my sister's apartment, and she didn't want to miss it. To this day, she insists I was never that sickly or in jeopardy of dying. She rationalizes this by explaining to me that if I were that sickly the hospital wouldn't let me call her, they would have called on my behalf. My father, who hates hospitals, came once and stayed for maybe five minutes. My sister never came, called, or asked about me. I later learned that she believed I was faking my illness because I was jealous of all the attention my dead brother was getting. I had no other visitors. I called to have the television turned on for myself. The TV and my team of doctors were my only contact with the outside world. First, my brother, and now this. It felt like caustic chemicals were being pumped into my body without my permission. I wanted to go home and hide from the world. When I was cleared for discharge from the hospital, my mother sent her sister to pick me up.

During the first year without Bryan, I was completely numb to everything, including holidays, so I didn't celebrate them. The second year hit me hard because I was no longer dissociated from my feelings, and I felt all the "firsts." By the third year, I still disliked the holidays and special occasions, but I had gotten to a point where I accepted that Bryan would no longer be a part of these occasions.

One morning I woke up to Buddy's cute little, graying face in mine, and things felt different. Buddy must have sensed it too because he jumped up and began wagging his tail. I hadn't seen him do that in quite some time. I imagine it was because he felt my pain and took on the responsibility of caretaker. Buddy was my lifeline throughout this entire struggle. He loved me unconditionally and never left my side. It was time for a change, and we both felt it. I began researching sibling loss. Sadly, I found very little. It was the least studied familial relationship from the point of bereavement. From the little I did find, I discovered we were referred to as "the forgotten grievers." Somehow giving it a name made me feel less alone. I read articles and books about grief and trauma. I learned that support was one of the most important predictors when it came to overcoming grief. This was something I lacked, so I increased my therapy to twice a week and learned what healthy relationships looked and felt like. He sincerely cared about the things I had to say and had been through. This unconditional acceptance and validation were new to me and something I didn't realize I so desperately needed. I began meeting with my parish priest on a biweekly basis. I began to heal. I developed a healthy and loving relationship with my father and his sister, Aunt Genie. I tried to reconcile with my mother's family but quickly remembered why I left their toxicity the first time. I learned to accept what happened to me and how I was treated by my family. I accepted it and moved on, establishing boundaries and releasing myself from toxic patterns. I discovered that it's not the people you anticipate that will be there for you but people you never expected that step up. Family is greater than simply sharing a bloodline. Friends are family that we get to choose. I became closer to Bryan's childhood best friend, Chad, and found peace and laughter in exchanging stories about him. Chad flew to New York so he could dance with me on my wedding day.

I slowly started to realize that my life wasn't over; it was just different. I began to fully accept that I had to rebuild my life, one that didn't include my brother. I began re-investing in this new life. I started opening my shades and letting the light in. I left the toxicity of hospital work and went into private practice, where I became my own boss. I learned alternative ways to self-care. I became certified in Reiki, tapping, mindfulness, and meditation. I started doing yoga and became involved with several charities and animal rescues. I began to experience positive emotions I never thought I was capable of. I got back into the dating world and met a wonderful man whom I married, bought a home with, and rescued several dogs with. We built a family. Together we found our spirituality and began speaking to the angels and Bryan. My GI issues subsided, and I was able to come off my medications. I now see a spiritual counselor as each day is another opportunity to discover who we are and how to grow.

This experience changed the way I perceive the world around me. I used to get angry when the car in front of me drove too slow or didn't hit the gas pedal as soon as the light turned green. Now I realize that the person in front of me may be struggling or having a bad day. I say this with absolution as I've been there. I've been the one honked at. It is hard to drive with eyes full of tears. I walk around barefoot as much as possible, especially outside. I enjoy feeling grounded and connected to the earth. This used to make me feel somber because my brother would never again feel the cool blades of grass bend beneath his feet. Now I realize it is because of him that I get to experience this. I take my time now. I'm more mindful and use all of my senses as opposed to just my brain. There's more to life than thinking. I follow my dogs around in the backyard. They have literally sniffed every spot and know the best places to venture off to. I now appreciate the feeling of a cool breeze across my face and don't worry about what it's doing to my hair.

Jack Lemmon once said, "Death ends a life, not a relationship." Over time I began to cultivate and strengthen that relationship with my brother. I used to feel like I was robbed of life when my brother died, but in reality, he set me free. I was living my life for my brother, always waiting for his next favor or phone call. He opened my eyes and showed me that the love I grew up experiencing was actually co-dependence. He taught me life is short and doesn't need to be so intense. In a way, I feel more loved by him now than I ever did before. He can see things clearly now from up above. I used to make daily trips to his grave, often sitting with him for hours. I've come to realize that I can speak to him whenever I want because time doesn't exist where he is. He's able to fully listen, undistracted from the nuances of day-to-day life. When I ask for signs of his presence, he always follows through.

Dealing with grief is like pushing a giant boulder up a steep mountain. It's something you have to continue to work at, but you get stronger and move forward more and more each day, month, and year. Yes, you will slip from time to time, and that's ok. Use that respite to acknowledge the work you've done and how far you've come, then find your footing and keep going. Don't be afraid to ask for help; you weren't meant to move that bolder alone. Grief never truly goes away. We learn to grow around it. And I wouldn't want it to go away. Grief is love. That hole in my heart represents someone I once loved and lost. You don't get over it; you get on with it. I did, and you can too.

When I was trying to decide whether or not to write my story, I asked my brother for a sign. The next thing I heard from the television was, "Think about how this will affect your brother." The same commercial repeated twice more before I told Bryan, "Ok, I got it!" My brother was a good man with a big heart who took great pride in helping others. He impressed me with his capacity to love and forgive. I chose to share my story in the hopes that it would be cathartic and help others see that there is life and love after loss. If this story helps just one person, then Bryan's life had a far greater purpose than he could have ever imagined.

Please note that some names have been changed for privacy purposes.

Here are a few things I found helpful along the way. Perhaps they can help you too.
- Surround yourself with those who have experienced or understand the grieving process.
- You will experience a multitude of emotions, and all of those feelings are ok.
- Don't listen to those who tell you how to grieve—there is no right or wrong way to grieve.
- You will learn who your true friends are and who really cares about your well-being. You may even be surprised by who steps up and who lets you down.

- Take it with a grain of salt when someone asks why you haven't moved on or come to peace with your loss yet—there is no time frame for healing.
- Be honest with yourself. If you don't feel like doing something, don't do it. You will get to it when it feels right.
- Try not to be offended when someone says the wrong thing. They meant well.
- Don't be afraid to ask for help or see a therapist.
- Don't listen when someone tries to compare your loss to one of their own. Grief is like a snowflake, and no two people grieve in the same exact way.
- Give it time. I know this has been said often about a lot of things in life, but when it comes to grief, it is absolutely true. Things do get better with time.
- Don't forget to take care of yourself. Self-care is paramount to healing.
- Don't make major decisions for at least a year. You don't want your emotions to interfere with your decision-making. Don't let your emotions control you. You need to control your emotions.
- Live in the moment and be kind. Tell people you love them. Don't go to sleep mad. You never know when something is coming to an end.
- You have five senses. Use them. There is more to life than overthinking.

CHAPTER 2

When I Need a Friend,
It's Your Name I Call

In loving memory of Faye Weisgal.
April 11, 1949 – May 27, 2022

By Patti Avin

There's such a hole in my heart that I can't seem to fill it with anything or anyone else. Maybe I don't want to or shouldn't try to. I
can't believe she's gone!! My mentor, my confidant, my best friend, my
go-to person, my sister! I feel so alone, even with all my friends and family
around. Almost seventy years of having her there for me, and I for her, have
now ended. My feelings of being lost and abandoned are overwhelming.

Faye and I grew up as only siblings in Far Rockaway, Queens, NY. Our
parents were on the verge of poverty, but we didn't have a clue. We shared
a room, played with toys, and had many friends. It was living together in
that room where we became best friends and confidants. We told each
other secrets, trusting each other that we would NEVER tell! We were
happy kids! We lived on the fourth floor of a New York City housing project. It was just two blocks from the beach, where we spent our summers.
It was a great childhood, which of course, we didn't appreciate at the time.
I have vivid memories of us laughing till all hours of the night in our beds
and our father coming in to tell us to "go to sleep and stop fooling around."

As we grew older, since both parents worked outside the home, Faye, being the Big Sister, had to watch me, which I know she sometimes resented. There were times when she ignored me, but she was never mean to me. When I was eleven years old and Faye was fourteen, we moved out of the city housing project and into the upstairs apartment of a two-family house in a middle-class neighborhood called Bayswater, Queens. Again, we shared a room and started really confiding in each other, as teenagers usually do with their best friends. I looked to Faye for guidance as I was becoming a teenager. Oh, boy, did we have secrets!

Faye meets Leo, marries, and Leo goes off to Vietnam. Faye moves back into our bedroom in Bayswater. She missed Leo terribly. I would hear her muffled cries as she buried her face in her pillow some nights, and my heart ached for her. As a family, we would gather around the radio and listen to the numbers of servicemen being killed over there day after day. When a letter arrived from Leo, Faye would read it first and then share with us the parts she wanted us to hear. I think this is when Faye found her spirituality. She used to say that "God may take my boyfriend, but he won't take my husband from me."

I walked with Faye every day to the mailbox to mail letters to Leo. Snow, rain, heat, nothing stopped her. She was more reliable than the mailman. When Leo came back from Vietnam, he was in a military hospital in St. Albans, NY. He needed minor surgery, so the Army sent him back to the states. I accompanied Faye to the hospital just about every day. I have considered Leo my Big Brother since I was fifteen years old.

Faye and Leo rented an apartment in Far Rockaway, Queens, and I stayed with them often. I was sixteen and needed to get away from my parents every now and then. Faye and Leo's was a safe place for me to run away to. When I married my husband, Mike, guess where our first apartment was? Yup, in the same building as Faye and Leo. We started having children, and they were brought up like sisters and brothers to their cousins. We were always together. Faye and Leo bought their first house in Levittown, NY, and a year later, Mike and I followed. Our house was less than a mile from theirs. We did EVERYTHING together as families.

I remember around this time, unfortunately, our parents were going through some issues with their siblings, arguing and fighting all the time. Faye and I were at our town pool with the kids, which we did very often, and we talked about our family's issues. We made a pact that we would never ever allow anything to come between us. If we disagreed on something, we would just agree to disagree and walk away. We toasted our drinks to it and flipped our pinkies, and so it was DONE!

My husband used to laugh because Faye and I, along with our kids, spent most days together, then Faye and I would leave for work as waitresses in the same Italian restaurant. We'd get home around 1:00 am, and by 8:30 am, we were on the phone figuring out what we were going to do that day. Mike would say, "You were with your sister all day yesterday. What could you possibly have to talk with her about on the phone at 8:30 am?" Too funny!!

In 2005, Faye and Leo sold their Levittown house and moved to another town on Long Island. Within a few years, they became snowbirds in Florida. Two of their children had already moved to Florida, so they wanted to be closer to their kids and grandsons. I was devastated when Faye told me about the move. Honestly, I didn't know how I was going to get through each day without her. I cried all the time! This was the first time we were ever apart from each other, and we would not be able to see each other every day. Faye told me that "things change," and we'll deal with it by visiting each other often and talking on the phone every day. In 2007, Mike and I followed our kids and grandkids to New England and bought a condo in West Warwick, RI. Faye and I remained regular daily phone buddies and visited each other as often as possible.

I'm telling you about our history growing up so you can really understand how close our families and we were. Our mother used to say how proud she was of her girls because they relied on each other so much and were there for each other. Friends of ours, who had strained relationships with their siblings, were envious. We definitely knew and were grateful for our relationship. But don't think for a minute that it wasn't a lot of work. Just like a marriage, you pick your battles and compromise if you love the other person, and the relationship is worth fighting for.

I spoke to Faye one morning in 2016 and told her I was suffering from vertigo. She said she was having the same issue. We both went to our respective doctors and shared each day what treatments we were doing to get rid of this debilitating problem. We compared exercises and medications. My vertigo was getting better, but Faye's wasn't. Eventually, she went to a balance clinic and an ENT doctor. Nothing was helping, so her ENT suggested a brain MRI just to be sure. It was January 2017 when Leo called me to tell me Faye had a brain tumor and needed surgery as soon as possible. I dropped to my knees and screamed! I was panic-stricken and felt like I was going to vomit. I immediately thought that Faye was going to die. I needed to be there for her, to comfort her, as we had always done for each other in the past.

I flew to Florida immediately. I remember on the plane feeling nervous, as if this was going to be the last time I'd see my sister. I quietly cried and sometimes sobbed the entire flight. When I arrived, Leo picked me up at the airport and filled me in on what was going on. Based on what he was describing, I dreaded seeing Faye and couldn't wait to see her at the same time. It was so horrible and scary watching Faye not being able to stand up straight, walking around, holding onto walls, and anything else she could lean against. She looked terrible and confided in me that she was scared. I told her I was scared too and would be there for as long as she needed. Crying became a regular part of my days. How could this be happening to my sister? To me?

I sat in the waiting room of Moffitt Cancer Center with Leo and their adult children. The doctor was optimistic but cautioned us that Faye might not be the same person when she woke up. I didn't really know what that meant, but I guess I was as prepared as I could be. I remember wishing I had long arms, like an octopus, so that I could wrap them around all of us. I was so scared for them and for me. Would Faye make it through the surgery? Would she know us when/if she came through? The anxiety level in the waiting room was so high I could feel it. The five of us sat most of the day in petrified silence. It was one of the longest days of my life. When our father was sick and dying, I clung to Faye. Same when our mother passed. Who could I cling to now? My husband, Mike, was there for me and very supportive, but I needed Faye! Without her, I felt very uncomfortable and almost terrified.

Hours later, after what I think was at least five trips to the hospital cafeteria, we were told Faye was out of surgery and doing okay. I held my breath waiting for the results. They removed a tumor and were testing it to determine if it was malignant and, if so, where the malignancy existed. We all burst out crying. We were so loud that I think people in the waiting room may have thought we were just told that our loved one had not made it out of surgery. The opposite was true, and I felt tremendous relief. Faye made it through the surgery!

Faye was so strong that she went home two days later. I stayed at her house to help her get around and give Leo a hand taking care of her. Her children came and went, but they had jobs and families they were responsible for. I know they were thrilled I was able to stay and help their father take care of Faye. She was amazing!! Mentally she was back to the "old" Faye, but just a little slower moving around. I changed her bandages, administered her medications, and did anything else she needed. Faye's son from NC came with his wife, and I went back to RI. Faye was doing great, and I felt comfortable leaving, knowing that I'd be back very soon.

Faye's brain tumor turned out NOT to be brain cancer, but metastatic lung cancer that had gone to her brain. I wasn't really sure what all that meant, but the big "C" word was enough for me to know this wasn't going to end well. I remember crying in my husband's arms when we got into bed that night. I was on such an emotional roller coaster, so happy her surgery went well but terrified that she wasn't going to live for very much longer. Selfishly I was thinking more about myself than her. How was I going to carry on without her in my daily life? At the time, I was really not thinking about how sick she was going to get. Now thinking back, I feel quite guilty about those feelings.

The doctors told Faye that if she had no treatment, she probably wouldn't live more than eight months to a year. So, of course, she and her family chose treatment. Chemo and radiation started, and she was doing great. We still spoke on the phone daily, and I visited as often as I could. I felt so helpless. Faye's positive attitude was getting me through my days. Calling her every day was supposed to be me supporting her, but it actually was the opposite. I needed her strength and encouragement to help me get through my day. I was far away, feeling scared and helpless. I could barely get through a conversation with her without crying. I apologized to her constantly as she consoled ME.

Faye was an artist by trade. One of only nine hand lace designers, I believe, in the country. She was a graduate of FIT (Fashion Institute of Technology) and extremely creative. When she started losing her hair from the radiation treatments, she purchased scarves and hats and always looked so "put together." She would wrap those scarves around her head or around the hats. Every scarf was a perfect match to her clothing, her shoes, and her purse. She should have been on the cover of a fashion magazine. She always looked so beautiful, and I felt proud of her for her courage and strength.

Faye and Leo had complete faith in her doctors at Moffitt Cancer Center. So, when she was told about a clinical trial, she immediately said yes. She told me that she was going to do everything and anything that would extend her life. After the first year, if she survived, better treatments would be developed, and she planned to take advantage of all of them. This was the BEST news! She was going to be OKAY, and my heart burst with happiness and pride.

Although her numbers and scans were good, after a few months of the trial, she developed pneumonitis and had to stop the trial. I knew she was disappointed, and I felt so frustrated for her. We hoped for a new trial down the road. As a result of the pneumonitis, she developed a terrible, debilitating cough. We would try to talk on the phone, but she couldn't get a sentence out without coughing violently. We had to send text messages instead. Some of the side effects from her treatments would have had most patients asking to stop treatment. She had sores in her mouth, so she couldn't eat. I felt so bad for her, knowing the misery she was experiencing. She lived on fettuccine alfredo and other soft foods. But she continued to go out for dinner because that was one of Leo's pleasures. What a fighter and a trooper, people would say. And they were right! She complained to me sometimes because she knew she could. We just had that kind of relationship, no judgment.

In 2018 Mike retired. I was a small business owner with a lot of freedom and flexibility. All I wanted was to be near Faye and spend as much time as I could with her. Traveling back and forth was becoming expensive, so I suggested to Mike that we could move to Florida. It was such an emotional struggle for me because I didn't want to leave my children and grandchildren. So, the next best thing would be to become "snowbirds" and spend three to four winter months in Florida and the rest of the year in RI near our kids.

In 2018, while visiting Faye and Leo, we went out for lunch with about four couples who were Faye and Leo's friends. I stood up and announced that Mike and I wanted to become snowbirds and rent a house in their community for the winter months. Does anyone know anyone who has a house for rent near Faye? One of the couples approached me and said that their house could be available because they usually go back to England for the winter. Done deal! We moved into our rental home in January 2019. I was ecstatic that we would once again be living near Faye and Leo. Just like old times!

In February 2019, Faye's scans showed another tumor in her brain that had to be removed. I think she was a little more nervous about this one because she had already lived past the timeframe they had initially given her. She came through that surgery as well, but I knew she was a little different. I noticed that she no longer seemed to have the spunk that she had before, and she was quieter, which made me very sad and deflated. She went home after only one night in the hospital. Her children were right there for her, as was I. I didn't want to leave to go back to RI. Spending time with Faye and helping her was all I wanted to do. However, Mike and I had to go back to RI in March 2019, but not before securing the rental house again for the winter of 2020.

I constantly thought about Faye. I was so far away and feeling helpless, but not hopeless. She had started maintenance chemo and was doing very well. Her cancer had spread, but her doctors were right on top of it. She was struggling with her constant coughing and other side effects, but she managed to get herself up and out each day. She had always been my hero. Now she was a Miracle!

All I could think of during the summer and fall months was getting back to Faye. I felt that I needed to be with her even more. I wanted to save her from all she was going through. Mike and I moved back to Florida in January 2020. We spent just about every day and night with Faye and Leo and their close friends. I would take Faye to some of her doctors and treatment appointments so Leo could play golf or go out to lunch with Mike and his friends. Then COVID hit!

Mike and I had already decided that we were going to look for a house to move to permanently in Florida. We loved the neighborhood and community and hated the cold winters back north. Our children and grandchildren were sad but understood why we wanted to move and that I needed to spend as much time with Aunt Faye as possible. I went to many open houses in the neighborhood looking for a house but eventually reached out to the couple we were renting from to ask if they wanted to sell us their house. We agreed on a price and went into a contract.

COVID prevented us from driving back to RI in March, as originally planned. We stayed in the house until May 15th and then drove back to RI to sell our condo and hopefully move permanently to Florida in December 2020. On June 25, 2020, while I was walking my dog, my phone rang. Faye's sons were on the phone and told me they had bad news. I immediately thought something had happened to Faye. I dropped to the ground in shock and burst into tears thinking the worst had happened. They told me that their father, Leo, had died suddenly. He was sitting in his chair watching TV and just died! OMG, I just lost my brother-in-law, and my sister is a widow! How could this happen? I had to be there for Faye. We flew back to Florida for Leo's funeral. I almost couldn't bear seeing Faye and her children, knowing and feeling the depth of their loss. It was devastating!

In August 2020, Mike and I became permanent residents of Florida, and my life shifted in so many ways. I became Faye's primary caregiver. I was a bit nervous about taking on the responsibility, but it was my pleasure to help her, as I know she would have done the same for me. I discussed with Mike how different our lives might be now that I was taking on this monumental responsibility and that I hoped he was still on my team. He embraced me and said he would help Faye and me however he could. I love this man so much!

Faye's cancer had spread more, and she was on the 3-month plan with Moffitt, which included maintenance chemo, radiation (if necessary), lung scans, brain MRIs, iron infusions, blood infusions, etc. This was our life, with an oxygen tank in tow. In between, we always tried to make time to grab lunch out if Faye felt okay or drop into a store to do a little shopping. Faye, at this point, was using a walker because the cancer had invaded her femur. As I watched her wince with pain, I felt so helpless. There was nothing I could do for her to alleviate her pain from the cancer and the pain of not having her Leo by her side.

At the end of each day, when I dropped Faye off at home, my heart broke for her as I watched her go into her empty house. I knew she missed Leo terribly, even though she didn't talk about him much. Whenever we talked about Leo, it was usually a happy or funny memory we had of him. Faye's children were by her side, there for her whenever she wanted, but they had jobs and families who also needed their attention. I know they were very thankful and appreciative that I was there for the day-to-day. They were good children, and I love them all.

For over two years, I was devoted to Faye. Sometimes I felt very uneasy and worried I wasn't doing things the way she wanted. She was still trying to be very independent and was vocal as to how she wanted things done. How her laundry should be done, where the dishes were kept in her cabinets, which lights in the house should be kept on and which ones should be shut off, etc. Although she thanked me constantly, I never felt completely confident. I felt tremendous guilt for leaving Mike so often to fend for himself. I'd pre-make dinners for him and stop off at the grocery store to ensure he had his diet coke and chocolate milk. Most days, I was exhausted by the time I put my head down on my pillow.

Again, Faye and I talked every morning. We talked about what we would do that day, what doctors or treatments we would drive to, what we would have for dinner, etc. I cooked dinner most nights and would invite her over. She would always ask, "What's for dinner tonight?" If she didn't like what I was making, she'd stay home and have soup or something easy. Most nights, though, she joined us for dinner. After dinner, we would watch "Family Feud," laugh at Steve Harvey, and then I'd drive her home. Most days, it was a nice ending filled with laughter.

We both took naps most afternoons. Faye sometimes took two naps a day. It was a routine, and we came full circle, back to living near each other and spending quality time together, sometimes laughing and sometimes crying together. Mostly I cried, and she laughed. She always teased me about being such a sensitive and emotional person. Faye loved butterflies and the color purple. We spent lots of time shopping for anything that had butterflies on it. Her toenail color was always purple. She felt it grounded her and made her feel powerful. The butterflies symbolized her breaking free.

We also talked about how wonderfully she was doing and how much time she had left to live. I promised her that when the time came when she didn't want any more treatments, I would not try to talk her out of it but would honor her wishes. I realize now that I didn't mean it completely. How could I just let her go? Selfishly I didn't want to be without her.

A few days after Mother's Day, where we spent a wonderful day at Faye's son's house eating and laughing with them, and Faye's two grandsons, Faye said to me, "Is this all worth it?" She was in pain, on so many pills, seeing so many doctors each week, and treatments upon treatments. She was just plain tired! I reminded her of the wonderful day we had just had, and how if she gave up, she wouldn't see her grandsons' smiles anymore. Was I supposed to say, "No, it's not worth it; it's time for you to give up if that's what you want?"

Wonder Woman was now completing her fifth year with cancer. She was tired but still managed to get up every day and do the best she could. The pain in her femur and lower back was excruciating, so a decision was made to start palliative care. I hated seeing her in pain and helping her with every step and activity she did. I was concerned that she wasn't taking her medication correctly, so I offered to set up her weekly pills for her. When she agreed, I was shocked. Faye is and was the most independent person I knew. She NEVER asked for help and fought it all the way. She was agreeable to being pushed in a wheelchair and became completely reliant on her walker, which was a good thing. We were all so afraid she would fall without the support.

Palliative Care. What does that mean? The doctor told me Faye was on her "downslope," and we needed to keep her as comfortable as possible. So, let's start her on some heavy-duty pain meds. Even my friend, a retired nurse, told me a Fentanyl patch would be the best thing for Faye at this point. Faye agreed to the pain patch, so we started every three days changing her patch. No pain!! This was wonderful! I hadn't seen Faye move around so well and smile so much in months. I don't know if "happy" was the right feeling I felt, but I definitely felt relief for her. This was a miracle!

Eventually, the patch stopped working well, so the doctor increased the dosage. That is when Faye's entire personality started to change, and I was worried. She would forget things, especially her medication. She couldn't walk without her walker again because she kept bumping into walls. She was supposed to be on oxygen 24/7 at this point, and I had to constantly remind her to put it on. She became a little belligerent and yelled at me a lot. I sometimes felt so angry I wanted to shout back, but I held my tongue and my rage. She would talk negatively about people to me, which she never ever did before. Faye usually gave people the benefit of the doubt and made excuses for what other people would call bad behavior. This was not the Faye I knew.

After a tough day with her, I would go home exhausted physically and mentally. Mike would ask me how the day went, and many times I would break down and sob, telling him how Faye was so rude to me and yelled at me. Although she ended each day with, "Thank you and I'm sorry," it was very hard for me to take without lashing back. I struggled with my feelings of resentment toward Faye. Here I was, giving so much of myself, and at times she acted as if she didn't care. I knew where it was coming from, and I accepted it, but it was still very hurtful.

I had to start going over to her house about an hour before she was to be ready for me to drive her to an appointment because she kept oversleeping. I'd wake her up and then direct her to the bathroom and help her get dressed, take her meds, eat a little bit (which she no longer wanted to do), and get out the door to the car. She gave me dirty looks and often screamed, "Stop rushing me!" I held my tongue and never responded or reacted to her outbursts. I felt frustrated and annoyed but kept it to myself.

One morning in mid-April 2022, while walking my dog, I passed Faye's house and saw that her outside lights were still on. This was a sign to me that she had not gotten up from bed yet, which was unusual for her by 8:45 am. I took a deep breath and went inside the house. My heart pounded so hard and fast that I felt dizzy. I called out to Faye, but no answer. The house was pitch dark. My biggest fear was in my throat. That vomit feeling again! I was petrified that I would find her dead in her bed. I walked slowly into her bedroom, and the bed was empty. I heard a faint sound coming from her bathroom and found her on the floor, wedged between the toilet and the wall. I called Mike, and he came over to help me get Faye up and back into bed. She was weak and couldn't really help when we tried lifting her up. She didn't cry or scream; she was just like a dead weight. This was the beginning of the next five weeks of what her doctors called her "downslope." I refused to accept that she was failing fast. I cried out of frustration because, once again, there was nothing I could do to stop this. I absolutely hated seeing her so weak and unable to even carry on a conversation. This was the day I realized I was losing the sister I knew and loved. I had so much compassion for her, but at the same time, I wanted to slap her back to herself. These thoughts now fill me with shame.

For the next nine nights, I slept on Leo's side of Faye's bed. She wasn't using her oxygen correctly or taking her meds correctly, and after her fall in the bathroom, I knew she needed constant care. I would set my alarm for every two hours to wake up to make sure she was sleeping and breathing okay. One time I woke up to my alarm, and Faye wasn't in bed. I jumped up and found her sitting on the kitchen floor. Poor thing didn't even remember how she got there. I called Mike at around 2:00 am to come over and help me pick her up off the floor and get her back to bed. Even though I was right there, doing the best I could, I felt so helpless. I was now also starting to feel hopeless. I realized she was not going to come back from this.

Faye passed away on May 27, 2022. After weeks of hospitalization, rehabilitation, and hospice care, she was gone. Our last conversation, if you want to call it that, was about Leo. She knew he was waiting for her. The Thursday night before she passed, I sat on her bed, stroking her arm and telling her how much I loved her. Her eyes were closed, but her mouth never stopped. She was mumbling, smiling, and had a confused look on her face. When I asked her who she was talking to, she opened her eyes big and wide, sat up straight, and very loudly said, "LEO!". She went to her beloved Leo on Friday morning at around 8:00 am.

Now what? I was so totally lost. I was experiencing every emotion I could think of all at once: devastation, loss, emptiness, aloneness, grief, love, relief, and even guilt. I was the only one left in my family, and I had nobody to call in the morning! The tears came hard and heavy like I had no control. Something took over my body, and I couldn't even collect my thoughts. I even felt annoyed at myself for moving to Florida. Life would have been much easier for me if I hadn't taken care of her. There would be less pain.

The next day when I awoke, I just lay in bed. I felt completely drained. This was my first day without Faye. My first day without speaking with her in the morning on the phone, with nowhere to go and no one to visit. It was over, and I felt so empty. I listened to music most of the day and just cried. "Wind Beneath My Wings" by Bette Midler was the hardest song for me to listen to. Faye and I had seen the movie *Beaches* together and cried like babies. I always told her that she was the wind beneath my wings. Why was I playing that song over and over again? It made me so sad but also made me feel so very close to Faye. She was definitely with me.

Faye's wonderful children took over. They arranged everything for Faye's funeral, and I really had nothing to do but sit with my thoughts and cry. And cry and cry and cry! I remember feeling so very lost, alone, and vulnerable. My husband was very compassionate, but really, there was nothing anyone could do for me. Faye was gone, and I had to deal with it. I was truly relieved that she was no longer suffering, and I knew she was where she wanted to be, but my heart was still broken, and I couldn't even think of a way to fix it. There was no miracle cure; it was just life—getting on with it and waiting for the pain to subside.

So very, many people reached out to me to send their condolences. It was so heartwarming knowing that so many people cared. Some people said the right things, and some said the wrong things. I don't think they intended to say the wrong things, but it just wasn't what I wanted to hear at that time. I KNEW she was in a better place; I KNEW she was no longer suffering; I KNEW she was a fighter, etc. I didn't need anyone to tell me that. The best were those who just hugged me and said they understood or those who just listened to me crying on the phone and said nothing. I'm writing this paragraph six months to the day after Faye's death, and I can only write about one sentence at a time. This is much more difficult than I had expected it to be. How do I explain all the feelings of reliving everything? Relief, resentment, bitterness, horror, and even joy with each word I write. I must constantly stop to wipe my tears or even walk away from the computer for a while.

I found it very hard to do some simple things that I used to do when Faye was alive. I couldn't walk my dog, Jelli, past Faye's house without wanting to walk in. Even Jelli turns to walk up the driveway when we pass the house. I couldn't listen to Sirius Radio '50s or '60s without hearing a song that reminded me of dancing with Faye or just being with her. Faye and Leo were amazing dancers, so the '50s Lindy music killed me. I could see them right in front of me, dancing up a storm. That vision should have made me smile, but it only made me sad. One of the hardest things for me to accept was not having day-to-day contact with my nephews and niece. Everyone gets on with their lives!

Anytime I saw a butterfly or anything purple, I'd totally lose it and start crying hysterically. I hated feeling like this, but I had no control. I started to create a playlist of songs that reminded me of our precious time with Faye and Leo. I don't know why I did that because I can't get through it without sobbing uncontrollably. The memories that flash in my mind sometimes make me smile, but knowing I have no one to share them and laugh about with is crushingly sad. I miss having Faye in my life and me being in hers. With each new thing that happens with my family, good or bad, I reach for my phone to text or call Faye to tell her. I always shared everything with her.

About two months ago, I bought the first book of this series and started reading each woman's story. I knew most of the women who contributed to the book, so it became even more interesting and closer to me. The main thing I took away from each story was how important it is to reach out for help if you're struggling with such deep grief. Other people had suggested that to me, but I dismissed it because I had always been a strong person and knew I would get through this in time. I was wrong!

I reached out to Moffitt Cancer Center in Tampa, Florida, where Faye had been a patient. I inquired about a grief group for the survivors of their patients. I needed help! I needed to talk with people who REALLY understood. I enrolled, and at the time of this writing, I have completed the eight weeks of group grief counseling. I purchased and am reading the wonderful book that the course is based on, *Understanding Your Grief,* by Dr. Alan D. Wolfelt. The grief counselor and hospice nurse who facilitate the group are wonderful. Listening to the other grieving survivors has been helpful to me. I'm not alone! There's actually a woman in the group who lost her older sister to cancer. The difference is she still has another sister to grieve with.

I've learned that everyone grieves differently. Grief is unique, and I must embrace the uniqueness of my grief. There's no right or wrong way to grieve, and I should NEVER be embarrassed or ashamed of grieving or outwardly mourning. I'm learning to nurture my grief and practice mindfulness. Being present in my feelings and allowing myself to feel the way I do at any specific time. I am not weak because I cry a lot. I just have so much love for Faye in me, with nowhere to go anymore.

Learning about unique grief enables me to be more understanding and accepting of how other people grieve or relate to a person in mourning. Many of the people I thought would reach out didn't. At first, I was hurt and angry, but as I learned more about the grieving process, I became more tolerant of how others might not be able to talk about their loss as easily as I could. Wanting to avoid everything and everyone associated with the loved one they lost. It was a real struggle for me at first because I didn't understand. But now I'm more comfortable and accepting of other peoples' unique grief. For me, denial is not an option. I want to be reminded constantly about Faye. I want to smile when I'm reminded or even cry, whichever releases me at the time.

I've planted a beautiful Bismarck Palm Tree in my backyard in Faye's memory. I have a purple heart with Faye's Jewish name, Faygala, inscribed on it, sitting under the tree. One of my neighbors gave me a red cardinal that I placed beside the heart. The way the branches fall out to the sides resembles a hug. Each morning, when I open my blinds, I say, "Good morning Faygala" as I give her a hug back and smile through my tears.

Faye had found spirituality earlier in her life, and I didn't necessarily get it. However, I've become more spiritual since I lost Faye. My newly found faith allows me to be more open and trusting. When we were cleaning out her house, I found some of Faye's books for daily reflection. I'm teaching myself to meditate and pray. Thanking the universe for everything I have rather than blaming it for everything I've lost. I feel much calmer now and have stronger feelings of serenity and joy. I speak to Faye often and am greatly comforted by doing so. I smile when I see a butterfly and paint my toenails purple. Every time I look down at my feet, I feel Faye's presence. I know she's where she needs to be, just as I needed to be by her side for those two and a half years. I hope I never stop crying because that would mean to me that I stopped loving. I'm so thankful Faye trusted me to take care of her, and I'm proud to have been able to do it. I'm going to keep her with me by continuing to learn from her. Her reflection books and her writings will guide me to become a more peaceful, serene, and joyous person.

Confronting the reality that Faye will never be physically in my life again is the hardest thing for me to grasp. But drawing on the experiences and encouragement of friends, fellow grievers, and counselors has helped me tremendously. I am forever changed by this experience. I feel that I have grown in my wisdom, understanding, and compassion. I'm still early in my grief process and look forward to the day when my sense of loss turns into remembrance of better times, and I'll smile without the tears instead of through them whenever I think of Faye. Memories still come so suddenly that they knock me sideways. I still sometimes fight to breathe, but I always let my tears flow.

In November 2022, with the help of some of Faye's closest friends, I put together a beautiful celebration of her life. We gathered at a pavilion in a lovely park. The tables were draped with purple tablecloths, and we had butterflies galore. One of Faye's friends showed up with a small canvas of a butterfly that she had painted early that same morning. It stood on a small easel stand on the table at the celebration. I brought some of Faye's scarves, hats, costume jewelry, etc., and asked that everyone feel free to take a memento for themselves. People stood up and spoke about how much they loved Faye and how she impacted their lives. I felt so very proud of my big sister and overwhelmed with joy as they talked about her, smiled, and shed some "love tears." We then walked to the lake, and each person threw flowers into the lake as we recited the Serenity Prayer. It was a beautiful day that I will remember for the rest of my life. Such support, love, and heartfelt compassion. I KNOW Faye loved it! The painted butterfly now hangs in my guest bedroom. I love looking at it as it makes me smile and reminds me of that wonderful day of celebration.

As I write this paragraph during the holiday season, 2022, I'm smiling as I remember celebrating Hanukkah with our family at Faye and Leo's house. I can see Faye hand-grating the potatoes & onions to make the most delicious potato latkes (pancakes). I can even smell the oil as if it were frying. I have Faye's recipe and will be giving it my best try. My playlist is playing, and I think I may be able to get through it this time. If not, I'll just keep trying.

I now set small goals for myself, like listening to my playlist without breaking down or walking Jelli past Faye's house. My next goal is to get to the cemetery to visit Faye. I've been on my way there three times, but I've turned back each time due to fear. Fear of what, I don't really know. It may be facing the reality that Faye and Leo are really gone. I dread seeing their graves side by side. I know I can do it and will when I'm ready.

Years ago, I gave Faye a gift that she hung in the office room of her house. It's a framed picture with a beautiful saying that is now hanging in my house.

Sisters and Best Friends
Time and Again
I choose you over all others
When I need a friend
It's your name I call

CHAPTER 3

Resilient Heart

In memory of the ones I've loved and lost.

Dylan J. Lambert: August 17, 1996 – September 9, 2015
Joseph J. Mariani Jr.: October 11, 1945 – October 8, 2016
Joseph H. Mariani: April 20, 1983 – August 2, 2018

By Gina Lambert

My family never talked about the tough stuff growing up. Our emotions were our own and were meant to be dealt with silently. We only discussed the easy stuff: the happy, fun stuff. My extended family was the same way. No difficult conversations: almost like it wasn't healthy to talk through things, process things, and learn how to move forward. I never witnessed my parents' feelings. No arguments. No sadness. Even during difficult times, no emotions. As I went through the process of writing and rewriting my grief story, I realized how much of that upbringing played into how I did not deal with my feelings in a therapeutic way throughout my journey until now.

On September 9th, a Wednesday night in 2015, I was sitting in my living room scrolling through television channels without focus while my two younger sons were playing video games in the basement. It was a school night, and pretty soon, I'd be yelling down to tell the boys it was time to get ready for bed. They were fifteen and thirteen years old. For my boys, it had been a typical school day in their world. It wasn't a typical school day for me. I had gotten a phone call at work that morning from my husband. He was crying, and I could barely understand him. He was calling to tell me that Dylan, his biological son, and my stepson had coded in a hospital in Las Vegas, but the doctors had gotten him back. He needed me to come home so we could figure out a flight for him and Dylan's biological mom to get to him, hoping to get there before it was too late.

So many thoughts raced through my mind on that car ride home. They came in rapid fire, and I judged just about every one of them. Are these the thoughts I should be having during a crisis like this? What should I be focusing on? Should I be crying harder? Who do I tell and burden this news upon? I just could not imagine calling my mom, dad, or even any of my friends to tell them what was going on. I didn't like seeing others suffer and certainly wasn't in a position to comfort anyone like I normally would. Do I take the boys out of school or let them have a "normal" day until they get home? I was scared and sad and had no idea how I was going to manage all of this for everyone around me. This was how I thought. Always about everyone else and not about myself. My husband always used to tell me that I worried too much. I would tell him that I couldn't help it. It was just something I had always done.

We had been here before. Dylan had been hospitalized several times in the last couple of years of his life in an attempt to deal with his mental health. We watched him struggle for the entirety of his life, and we did all we thought we could do to support him along the way.

At 8:30 pm that same day, I got a phone call from my mother-in-law. She was wailing. Dylan was gone. I had to ask her to repeat herself. It didn't feel real. I didn't think I had heard her correctly. And I certainly did not know how to feel. My first thought? "It's over. The pain, the suffering, the struggles, the worry." My second thought was, "How do I tell Dylan's two brothers that he is gone?" I was panicking on the inside. My heart was broken, and I felt empty. I was scared, devastated, and unsure of what to do next. My whole body was shaking and numb all at the same time. I wasn't crying yet. No one talks about how you tell your children that their brother is gone. What words do I say? How do I start explaining what happened? Do I have them sit down and "break the news gently?" What the hell does that even mean? Do I just come out and say, "Your brother is gone? Dead?" I just could not figure out the "appropriate" way to tell them he was gone. It was just the boys and me. I had never felt more alone in my whole life, and I will never forget each of their responses as I explained that they would never see their brother again.

One ran into my arms crying, while the other ran out onto the deck and screamed at the top of his lungs. True devastation. My heart broke for a second time within ten minutes. First for Dylan and then for his brothers. How I felt at that moment did not matter. I was an adult and would have to deal with my feelings at a more appropriate time. Remember, we did not discuss feelings when I was growing up, especially during the tough times. I wanted better for my own children, so I knew I needed to be sure to be open and ready to communicate with them. I wanted them to be able to talk with me about anything because I did not have that experience as a kid. The part I didn't factor in was that it was just as important for me to take care of myself at the same time.

The boys and I spent that night crying, looking through years of pictures, and reminiscing. We did all we could to distract each other from the devastation that we felt. Sleep did not come easily and did not last long. Our relationships changed that night. Before this tragedy, it was my job as a mom to protect and care for my children. Now the boys felt and showed a need to do the same for their dad and me. My innocent, sweet, caring boys were suddenly young men. I just could not imagine what losing a brother felt like. And to lose him so young and so unexpectedly. Our world turned upside down.

I wasn't sure what was supposed to happen next, and I questioned every decision I made. I tried to keep things as normal as possible, although I wasn't sure what "normal" was anymore. Besides taking one son for an oral surgery appointment the following morning, I also went to my dad's first oncology appointment. I went through the motions in a fog. Keeping my emotions in check was not easy, and looking back, it was also unhealthy. Every muscle in my body was tense and on edge. I was in a constant state of nauseousness and could not eat. My nerves were frayed, and this deep, hollow feeling had taken over. I felt that I needed to be okay for my family. They needed me to be strong for them. Being strong for others was something I was really good at and had done all of my life. Was I okay? Most definitely not. The boys' mental health became my mission in life. I'd be damned to go through this again with a second son.

The next couple of weeks were overwhelming in many ways. We were surrounded by so many amazing family members and friends I consider family. People dropped off meals, sent messages and prayers, and checked in on us regularly. I went back to work, and the boys went back to school. Every day was a challenge. I made sure the boys had a connection with the psychologist at each of their schools, and we talked daily about whatever they needed or wanted to talk about. I know I wasn't sleeping well, nor was I eating much, but I really can't remember doing anything, in particular, to help myself in my depth of sorrow. I did my best to take my own grief and lock it away in the back of my mind to deal with later. I had too many people depending on me to worry about myself.

My coworkers were equally amazing. They checked in on me and always asked how I was doing. My response was usually, "I am doing okay." It was easier to say that than to actually think about it and then verbalize how I was feeling on the inside. One very dear coworker took me to get matching semicolon tattoos on our fingers, as I had mentioned to her it was something I had wanted to do. This was the one special thing that I did for myself in memory of Dylan. This tattoo helps me to keep Dylan close in some small and powerful way. He was my baby boy, even though I did not give birth to him. I like the symbolism of the semicolon being a pause when things get rough instead of a period which would symbolize an ending. It's my little reminder that even when life gets tough, we can step back, take a breath, seek help if needed, and then keep moving.

As you may imagine, Dylan's memorial service was very emotional. I stood at the end of the receiving line, surrounded by family members who gave me comfort. One of those family members was my dad. He was wearing a suit that was too big and just hung on his shrunken frame. It was too big because he was sick. Over the past few months, he had lost several pounds and had been in and out of the hospital. We were beginning the process of walking through his cancer treatment. He sat there quietly, stoic even, which was my dad's personality forever and ever. He wasn't one to show much emotion, but I could see that he was hurting too. It made me sad to see him so small and unwell.

Hundreds of people came to pay their respects that day. My boys were overwhelmed by the number of friends who came to support them and cry with them. The support was truly incredible. I know we went to dinner after the service with family. I do not remember much of that night. The whole thing was exhausting. I was trying to keep it all together, all the while supporting my husband, who was suffering dearly, and most importantly to me, watching over my boys, being sensitive to their needs, trying to push them just enough to create a new normal, and not too much that they shut down. I felt as though I was constantly walking on eggshells so as not to disturb the delicate balance of what we were holding together. It was so exhausting.

My body was in a constant state of fight or flight. Always looking over my shoulder for something else to go wrong, making things even harder than they already were. Any small upset could tip the whole ship, and I knew I would not be able to cope with that, which scared me desperately.

We continued on with life to the best of our abilities after Dylan's memorial. My husband was out of work for about six months. The boys were back in school, regularly seeing the school psychologist and refusing to go to counseling outside of school. They continued on with their sports and activities. I felt that them being busy and preoccupied would help them through the hurt. I was so sad that this was their teenage life, dealing with the loss of their brother. I felt compelled to make things as seamless or easy as possible to try to compensate for all they were dealing with. Meanwhile, I just chugged along, keeping my grief to myself. Crying in private and not talking to anyone about my thoughts or feelings.

I hated crying, but anytime I allowed myself to let go and sit in my feelings, I would cry. This crying was gut-wrenching, snot-producing, blubbering crying, and what I would call ugly crying. It would leave me with puffy eyes and a pounding head, and I didn't have time for that. It was like living in complete isolation. A private grief bubble that I did not let anyone into. At all. I felt I had to. While grieving this huge loss, I was also going to doctor's appointments with my dad, asking questions and making sure he was getting the best care possible during his treatment.

In April of 2016, seven months after we lost Dylan, I drove my dad and his new wife to Boston to talk about scheduling surgery to remove my dad's tumor in his pancreas. He had gone through several months of chemotherapy, and we were hoping the scans would show a reduction in the size of his tumor. The ride to Boston was pleasant and light-hearted. We thought we were gearing up for a new beginning for my dad. The conversation revolved around what dad's life would look like after surgery. He planned to go back to work after he recovered. And start biking again, which had been his obsession for the last decade or so. Back to normal was what we were looking for, but sometimes things never go back to normal.

Sitting in the oncology doctor's office, the doctor reviewed the scans that were completed. Although my dad's pancreatic tumor has shrunk, his cancer metastasized to other organs in his body. The energy in the room changed, and I felt physically sick. I could not take a deep breath or say any words. I had those unpleasant butterflies in my stomach and thought I might need to run to the bathroom at any second. I kept quiet, focusing on my breathing and taking in my dad's body language as he digested this development. After a minute or two, he asked the doctor what he should do next. His doctor was simply amazing. He was so caring and empathetic, and real all at the same time. He told my dad to take out that bucket list of things he had been wanting to do and start doing them. He told my dad to enjoy every minute he had left of his life. And that is what my dad did. He rode his bicycle around the parking lot of his condo complex. He went to car shows. He took day trips to places that brought him joy. He tried to do as many things on the list as his body would allow.

I spent more time with my dad during that last summer. We talked about what life would be like without him. He worried about all of us. I reassured him that we would take care of each other and be okay. I was grateful that we had had so much time with my dad after his pancreatic cancer diagnosis. Most people don't live that long. I hated watching him suffer and be in constant pain. No one wants to see a loved one suffer like that.

During this summer of appreciating life's precious moments, my brother had major open heart surgery to replace valves in his heart for the second time within a couple of years. This second surgery gave him a five percent chance of survival. My brother was only thirty-three years old. Since he was born, we have always had a very close connection. I often tell people I was his second mom. I was so scared for him and felt helpless. Again, those feelings had to be stuffed away in that locked compartment.

My mom, my dad, and my kids needed me. Someone had to look over them and make sure they were handling things to the best of their abilities. I felt the weight of the world on my shoulders, never realizing that I could not be responsible for other people's happiness.

Thankfully, my brother survived this second surgery. It was truly miraculous. I visited my brother often during that hospital stay. Open heart surgery is gruesome, and the recovery is very painful, long, and difficult. One day while I was visiting my brother, my very sick dad appeared in the hospital room doorway. He and my brother had had a very strained relationship since my brother was a teenager. I was livid that my dad had come. And I told him so. I was worried that he would get sick. A sickness that would probably kill him. He looked at me and laughed.

Despite my fear of my dad's failing health, it was heartwarming to see my brother and father talking. My dad offered the olive branch, and my brother took it. The sadness I felt knowing that my dad's time was short and he and my brother had missed out on so much together over the years almost pushed me over the edge. These two men were such important people in my life. I wanted to scream at the top of my lungs, "Why our family, God?! What did we do to deserve so much agony and heartache?"

In September 2016, a year after we lost Dylan, Dad's body began to shut down. He needed his abdomen drained a few times as it began repeatedly filling with fluid. I knew from experience that this was a sign of the end coming sooner rather than later. On one of these occasions, I was driving Dad and his wife home. My dad was in the front seat with me, and his wife was in the back seat. He was talking to me about what he'd be leaving behind and how it should all go to my mom. Dad was very organized and practical. We had already talked through all of the logistics of his material things and how they were to be dealt with. It was a very uncomfortable conversation with his wife sitting in the back seat. He didn't know what he was saying. That's when I knew we were near the end. Mentally preparing myself for this moment had been a long time coming. As much as I knew I would be devastated by the loss of my dad, I also knew I would feel relief that he was no longer living in constant pain. I felt grateful for all of our long, open, and honest talks and the precious time that we had together.

The first week of October came, and it was time for hospice to step in and support my dad at home. I didn't want him to die in a hospital, and he didn't want that either. My dad was not a religious person and was very afraid of dying. It broke my heart. Over these last few months, we had several heartfelt conversations. It's funny how the reality of death helps people open up and talk about how they really feel. I am very grateful for that time I had with my dad. We were already close, but that time brought us even closer.

One fall night, while sitting in my driveway, I was on the phone with my cousin, telling her about the hospice plan. As we talked, I was overcome with this beautiful smell. A smell that I cannot describe, nor do I recall what it smelled like. It was a smell that surrounded me. I walked up and down my road thinking it was someone's dryer sheet and that I could find the source. The smell followed me all the way up and down my road. Once back home, I said goodbye to my cousin and then called my youngest son to come outside and smell this beautiful smell. When we got back outside, it was gone. At that moment, I realized the smell was a message. A message from my grandmother, my dad's mom. This was a woman I had never met but knew so much about because my dad had told me so many stories over the years. She had died of ovarian cancer before my parents had even met. He missed her dearly. That smell was her letting me know she was here, ready to help my dad cross over.

When I sat with Dad, his wife, and the hospice nurse in his living room the next day, I told him the story of the beautiful smell. I let him know his mother was here waiting for him. He broke down and cried. I only hoped that it would give him some peace during this whole process.

I sat next to my dad that day on his loveseat while a crew came in with his hospital bed. I rested my head on his bony shoulder with my arm around him, and he said to me, "Wow, this is really happening, isn't it?" I replied, "Yes, Dad. It is." We sat in silence while the bed was put together. I couldn't imagine the thoughts and feelings my dad had at that moment, knowing that this was the end for him. I wanted to do everything in my power to keep him as comfortable and safe as I could. I stayed at my dad's for the rest of that week to take care of him. His wife was too emotional to do it. He was on a strict regimen of medications to control his pain. He was so afraid to die in pain. I wasn't going to let that happen.

On Friday, October 7th, my dad took a turn for the worse. He wasn't eating or drinking anymore and slept the day away. I made sure that everyone came to say their goodbyes. His best friend, who lived in Georgia, even drove up that Saturday to say goodbye. It was a very emotional day for all of us. It was so hard to watch the people who loved my dad say goodbye. My sisters came and went. They couldn't handle seeing my dad like that. We all deal with death differently, and I completely understood how they felt. I, on the other hand, felt that I could not leave. I needed to see him through this transition, not just for him. But for myself as well. I guess the best way to explain it is that helping him through this transition helped me find some peace in it as well. Knowing, seeing, and experiencing Dad peacefully moving from one world to the next comforted me.

That night, my mom, Dad's wife, and I settled in for a night with Dad. We thought it would be his last. I wasn't prepared to say a final goodbye to my dad. I could not imagine living my life without him. No more long Sunday bike rides discussing life's challenges and critiquing the articles we would both read in bicycling magazines. No more kids' sporting events together or birthdays, holidays, or family cookouts. At the same time, looking at his withered body and his constant pain without medication, I knew I had to let him go. I crawled into bed with him, kissed his cheek, and whispered in his ear, "Dad, everyone who came to say goodbye has come and gone. You don't have to hold on anymore. It's okay to rest easy now." I kissed him on the forehead and then settled into his recliner.

Dad died peacefully that night without pain while holding my Mom's hand. I didn't cry. I lovingly assisted the hospice nurse in washing his body and preparing it for the funeral home. It was peaceful and an honor to do that for him. I went home that night having to tell my boys that their Grampy had died. Both of them hugged me, told me they loved me, and went back to bed. My dad was my best friend. I never thought twice about caring for him through his cancer diagnosis and his death. Sleep came swiftly that night. Having been at attention and ready to do anything my dad needed for the past several months had taken its toll on me. I welcomed the sleep.

My pain and grief continued. That compartment in my mind where I had stuffed all of my loss and grief was bursting at the seams. I struggled to sleep and eat. I got up every day and went to work and did all the mom things while I was numb inside. I felt like a robot and kept a smile on my face. Many nights I would sip on some rum or take a sleeping pill just to get some rest. It was a very hard time for me. On one of these nights, my dad came to me in a dream. I am not one to remember my dreams once I have woken up. There are just a handful of dreams that I remember. This was one of them. I still remember it like it happened last night. I was in the market carrying a huge bag of dog food. My dad was standing at ease in the checkout line. He smiled when he saw me but never moved. I dropped the big bag of food and gave him a big hug. While I held him in that hug, he thanked me for taking care of him and said he was sorry that I had to see him that way. It was a very peaceful and heartwarming dream. It gave me comfort.

I knew that I needed to find a way to help myself grieve, so I began going to a Spiritualist Church in East Providence that some friends recommended. I've always felt a connection with the other side. I know we have guides in our lives that watch over us. I talked to my dad often after his death (and still do to this day). And sometimes I can hear his responses, in his own voice, in my head. I found this church to be immensely helpful. The energy in the room was always peaceful and light. I had grown up going to church, so it was comforting to be in a space where people supported each other, laughed and cried with each other, and prayed together. I went regularly and learned how to meditate and breathe. I learned that it was very important to take care of myself. Reiki, essential oils, and crystals became part of my daily practice. It was a slow and gentle learning curve. It was the beginning.

Four months after my dad died, my dad's best friend's (who drove up from Georgia to say goodbye) son overdosed. He was still alive but brain-dead. These people are my family. We spent Christmas Eve together every year, birthday parties, weekends, etc. I always refer to them as my cousins because family isn't always blood. At the same time, my brother was in the hospital again with an infection. Anytime he got an infection, he ended up in the hospital due to his very fragile health. My cousins were in charge of working out a plan to donate their brother's organs. Their parents weren't able to make the trip from Georgia before their son was taken off of life support, so I went to support them. My cousins, my brother, and I all stood around my cousin while a priest prayed over him. We held his hands and cried quietly while they rolled him away to harvest his organs. It's what families do for one another.

At this point in my story, my marriage was falling apart. My husband was not supportive of me being upset about my cousin. He wasn't supportive of me dealing with losing my dad. I don't think he had the mental capacity to empathize with me. He was still struggling with the loss of Dylan, as we all were.

In March, we separated while still living together. It was a very contentious time. I was just destroyed. Everything I thought about my life and how I planned to live had blown up in my face. My family was torn apart. I cried. I cried a lot. I spent much of my time with friends trying to process and make sense of what was happening to me. It did not feel real. He moved out in June 2017. The boys went to live with their dad. They told me they knew I would be okay. I reassured them that I was okay, although I wasn't okay. I didn't know who I was anymore. I had dedicated my life to my family — my boys. I was a mom before anything else. I hadn't lived by myself without people to care for in twenty years. I questioned how to move forward.

During this time, a dear friend brought me to a medium. She felt it would help me connect with loved ones who have passed. The medium already had a page of notes for me when we arrived. The messages were from my dad and his mom. They were together again. My dad told me that he was happy and healthy and would have come sooner if he had known how good it was on the other side. He also told me that I deserved to be happy and brought Keith to me because he was a good man. Keith was a friend I had met at softball a couple of years before. It was an unexpected relationship that grew out of friendship after my husband left. Dylan also came through in that reading. He told me he knew how much I loved him and that he was working through all of his problems and making a lot of progress. It was a very emotional reading, and I had not cried that hard in quite some time.

The reading gave me hope. I was struggling so much with everything. I worried incessantly about my kids. I felt like I had failed them as a mom.

I never intended for our lives to fall apart the way they had. I really felt like I had ruined their childhood. I couldn't imagine having to leave my childhood home that was filled with so many memories while also grieving the loss of a brother and a grandfather and now life as they knew it. My boys were so amazing and resilient. We talked openly about how we felt about everything going on. I often saw them trying to protect me in the same way I always tried to protect them. What did I do to deserve such amazing young men?

The next year created a new normal for all of us. We sold our house, and I moved in with Keith. The boys continued to live with their dad and do typical teenage stuff. We had many conversations about feelings and new expectations with our new normal. Holidays were difficult being separated. We got through them. They had been through so much in their short lives. I could not even imagine it because I continued to feel sorrow and culpability for my boys' broken lives. I still was not focused on myself and my own healing process.

The next summer, my brother texted me that he was back in the hospital with another infection. He sent me pictures of his swollen hand and arm. He also sent me a picture of the song he was listening to: "Danny's Song" by Loggins & Messina. We both loved music and often connected through music. I asked him to keep me posted and told him I loved him. I didn't go visit my brother in the hospital this time. It was very hard to see him so sick, and he had been in and out of the hospital so many times that he was over it. He could be really cranky and rude to everyone around him. I didn't have the energy for it that week.

On August 2nd, 2018, I had come in from mowing the lawn and was getting ready to go to my volleyball game. I saw that I had missed a phone call from my brother's mother-in-law. I called her back. She was sobbing. My brother had died. He got up from his hospital bed to go use the bathroom and collapsed. The doctors couldn't revive him. He was 35 years old. He was my favorite sibling. I was devastated all over again. I felt guilty for not having gone to visit him that week. I was sad that I wasn't there for him when he died. I wasn't holding his hand and telling him it would be okay. I didn't get to be part of that transition as I had been for my dad. It broke me.

Pushing my broken feelings aside, I had to figure out how to tell my Mom that her only son was gone. I drove to my mom's house, playing and replaying over and over in my head how I would tell her that her only son had died. How could this be happening? Why was it happening to us? What did we do to deserve so much devastation over the past few years? How would we make it through another loss? How would I carry the load of another loss for my family? I was the "fixer" in the family and felt it was my job to make everything better for everyone else, leaving the leftover crumbs for myself.

I walked into my mom's house. She was surprised to see me. She said, "What is it?" She could tell by the look on my face that something bad had happened. I told her that Joe was gone. She cried briefly. Then she pulled herself together, because that's what we do, and came with me to tell my boys more devastating news. My mom and I sat at the kitchen table with my two boys. We told them their uncle was gone. They both just sat there thinking, feeling, and shedding some tears. My youngest son looked at me and said, "I know what it's like to lose a brother Mom. If you ever need to talk, I am here for you." It took everything in my being not to break down and completely lose it.

My mom and I left my boys and went our separate ways. I drove straight home and got in the shower. This is where I lost my shit. That locked compartment inside of me burst. It all came pouring out like Niagara Falls. I cried and cried and sobbed in waves for I don't know how long. While sobbing in the shower, someone was knocking on the bathroom door. I just ignored it. I figured it was Keith having come home from his softball game. When I got out of the shower, I saw that Keith was texting me, asking where I was. I told him I was just getting out of the shower and asked if he wasn't there at home. No, he was still at softball. I was confused. Who was knocking on the bathroom door? I walked the whole house looking for a human being, but there was no one. That's when I realized that my brother was knocking on the door while I hysterically sobbed in the shower. He was with me and wanted me to know that he was still here. Through my complete breakdown, I felt a bit of peace. Even though he was gone, we were still connected.

When I think back on all that I have been through since 2015, I wonder how the heck I made it through. I know I still have a lot to process and work through. My boys are grown now and making lives for themselves. Until recently, I struggled to "cut the umbilical cord." I felt so much guilt around the divorce and leaving them. But I now realize that I did not leave them and was always there for them. I spent so much time trying to make their lives "good" because they deserved better. Of course, we all want better for our kids. Now I know that this is their journey. They come to me for advice and to talk about life experiences. Ultimately they make their own decisions, and that is okay! It is NOT my job to make them happy or to make sure they have good lives. That is their job. My job is to continue to be here for them, support them, pray for them, and love them as I always have.

Now it is my time to take care of myself. I have started therapy. While writing my journey of grief, I came to realize how much I have not dealt with and how it is slowly eating me alive. I am excited about the process of going through therapy. I know it will be painful and difficult. That is okay. I look forward to actually feeling so much that I had stored away in that compartment in my brain and heart for so many years. One thing I am beginning to understand about myself is that I would never just sit in my emotions. Allowing myself to truly feel my emotions empowers me to address each emotion, understand why I am feeling it, and deal with it effectively. When you take the time to work on yourself, amazing things will happen.

I also find solace in running. It is a great space for me to think freely and listen to music or podcasts. Running boosts endorphins and is my physical release for so much pain. Connecting with nature always helps me to ground myself as well. Breathing in the fresh air, hiking on a trail, or sitting by the water allows me to clear my head. These are the times when I talk to the people that I love on the other side. I look for signs from them. I find comfort in knowing that they are together in this next phase, and I only hope their connections are strong and positive.

We never know what someone is going through in their life, and it's important to be mindful of that. We make it look like we have it all together when realistically, we are crumbling on the inside. That old saying, "Don't judge a book by its cover," has a different meaning to me now. Sometimes it takes all our effort to just make it through the day and do the things that are expected of us. When people who don't know me well hear my story or even just a small piece of it, their response is usually, "I would never guess that you've been through so much." So when someone is out of sorts, seems "off," or treats you in a not-such-great way, know that they may be having a hard time in their life and could use a break. We are all just trying to do our best.

I don't know why some of us suffer more loss than others throughout our lifetime. I do know that I want to use my experiences to help others. Talking about what I've been through and how I am figuring out how to process it all might just be what someone else needs to hear. I know I could have benefitted from stories of others suffering and how they made it through years ago. If I can help even one person not feel alone and see that life can go on, then it is all worth it.

My promise to myself is to continue working on myself through therapy, writing, talking to others, striving for my dreams, loving hard, and living my best life. Now I know I deserve it and am worth it. Do not struggle by yourself through loss of any kind. Seek support. Find what works best for you. Know that you are not alone and there is always someone, somewhere, who wants to support you.

Here is what I have learned about grief because of my experiences:
- Grief comes in waves and can hit you unexpectedly at any time.
- Grief doesn't end, but it changes as the years go by.
- Everyone experiences grief at some point in their lives.
- Grief experiences can be big or small, but they ALL matter.
- How you work through your grief may not work for someone else.
- Learning strategies to use during waves of grief help to minimize its impact.

I will leave you with a poem I found on my dad's corkboard after his death.

Tis the human touch in this world that counts,
The touch of your hand and mine,
Which means far more to the fainting heart
Than shelter and bread and wine,
For shelter is gone when the night is o'er,
And bread lasts only a day,
But the touch of a hand and the sound of a voice
Sing on in the soul always.
—S.M. Free

CHAPTER 4

A Letter to My Son

In loving memory of eugeNE emIL (NEIL) Fachon III
May 8, 1996 – February 19, 2017
"Never underestimate the power you have
to touch someone else's life." —Neil

By Wendy Nadherny Fachon

Dear Neil,

Over the past five years since your passing, I have often thought about how you came into my world and how you left it, with an astonishing symmetry, like two bookends holding a precious collection of stories in between.

You were in a hurry to enter this world, and I was impatient to greet you. After just an hour of labor in the delivery room, attended by a midwife, there you were! A miracle! I remember your first breath, holding your small body in my arms for the first time and feeding you at my own breast. Such comfort and joy.

When Dad and I brought you home, the thing we worried about most was how well your eyes would track and how good your eyesight would be. I wrote about that in your Baby's Record book, and now think, "How uncanny that we worried about your eyes back then." I had written down all your celebratory milestones—your first smile at five weeks, sleeping through the night at ten weeks, your first tooth at four months, and that sharp nip around five months that put an end to breastfeeding.

We propped you up in a high chair with a tray of Cheerios and watched you master your fine motor skills. You were sitting up on your own at six months and crawling one week later. At nine months, you took your first steps, eleven in a row, on Valentine's Day.

Your first words were "Up" and "Down." So, I would pick you up and hug you, and then, at your command, I would set you down and let you get on with your life. Rather than defying us with the word "No," you used the word "Why." You were an old soul on a quest for answers, reason, logic, and possibility. Watching both you and your sister grow and thrive gave me the greatest joy.

Then, Dear Soul, at the age of nineteen, you began leaving my world in the reverse order of how you came—losing your ability to walk, your fine motor skills, your ability to speak clearly, and your smile. I will forever mourn the loss of your smiling face: your heart-warming smile, your goofy smile, your devilish smile, your angelic smile, your smug smirk, your "over the moon" grin, your silly "Squirrel Boy" face, your infectious smile. Smiling was your natural state of being. You were my Jester, and then cancer took it all away.

Why were you the one to be diagnosed with a cancer deemed aggressive, inoperable, and incurable at age nineteen? Why not me? I would have exchanged places with you in a heartbeat. That's how much I loved you. I was approaching retirement age, and you were just reaching the prime of your life. Everything was out of order.

Your second year of college had been going so well until you sent us that email detailing three concussions you had suffered in a period of three months. You wrote:

"For the past 3 weeks I have been having difficulty with my vision. I'd had a little bit of difficulty after the first 2, but it wasn't too bad and I figured it would get better. On a day to day basis I am relatively fine, but when doing physical activities I get double vision. The more strenuous the activity the worse my focus."

You went on in your email to make light of the situation, explain what you were going to do about it, and assure Dad and me that you were okay. Still, we were worried. That is what parents do, and that is why we pressed you to request an MRI. We were right to be worried. Five months later, after new symptoms appeared, you were finally sent for an MRI, the results came back, and we were told you were dying of DIPG—*diffuse intrinsic pontine glioma*—terminal brain stem cancer.

Neil, I was unable to accept this. It was impossible. I went numb. While watching your face and posture transform through the initial emotions of shock, realization, panic, despair, and sorrow, I suppressed my own feelings. You had been studying the brain with fascination in Psych class and on YouTube. Did you know the brain can protect the body from trauma by activating the release of hormones, *endorphins*, which numb painful emotion? I think that is what happened to me. At the same time, my body began producing *epinephrine*, the survival hormone, and my mama bear fight instinct kicked in. I needed to be brave and strong. I was preparing to defeat the beast inside your head and save you.

You grew up with an eagerness to tackle impossible tasks, and this one was the height of impossible. After the initial shock, you called forth a determination to overcome *this* challenge while I stepped away from my youth work and writing commitments to devote all my time to you, uncertain how much time we had left to be together. We were aware of the limitations of conventional medicine, and you were open to exploring alternative modalities. You welcomed my suggestions for the integrative support of a colonic hydrotherapist, a community herbalist, a naturopathic oncologist, and energy healing practitioners. Medical marijuana? Bring it on. We tried anything and everything that made logical sense to us, turning the challenge into quite a story!

I joined two Facebook groups—*DIPG Awareness for Family and Friends* and *DIPG Research*. The membership included parents of children undergoing radiation, parents sharing experiences with natural therapies, parents seeking the newest experimental treatment, parents giving updates on their child's treatment, and parents losing or having lost a child to the disease. It was a place where hope battled mightily with despair. Every family came there in search of a support network and a cure.

Like one of your speed games of chess, we had to make our moves quickly. Dad started looking through the federal government's clinical trial database and was already familiar with the Burzynski Clinic in Houston, which happened to be starting a trial that was DIPG-specific and did not require prior radiation. You and Evie went online and managed to find Celeste, an adult DIPG survivor from Argentina, who had been cured by that same clinic. You connected with Celeste and found hope in her remarkable story. Encouraged by this synchronicity of events, we flew down to Houston, where the invincible Dr. Burzynski led us into an epic battle on multiple fronts.

Moving forward, your positive energy, dauntless spirit, and scientific reasoning were put to the ultimate test, but somehow, you managed to face every setback with an admirable attitude. Suddenly finding yourself back under the care of your parents is not where you were supposed to be. You had hopes and dreams for the future that were being shaken apart. You missed your college friends and campus life. Life at home was dull after all the excitement of school activities and interactions. While you adjusted to life with a much slower pace, Dad, Evie, and I did our best to liven things up without overdoing it.

Neil, how grateful I am for all the happy memories we made as a family in Houston ... basking in the joyous atmosphere of Ruggles Green while waiting for a table ... donning white lab coats and touring the Burzynski Institute pharmaceutical production facility ... exploring the NASA history and newly emerging technology at the Johnson Space Center ... watching the spectacle of thousands of bats emerging at twilight from beneath a bridge in the center of the city ... learning how to play the cooperative board game Pandemic in our hotel suite.

When irrational forces and unforeseen obstacles tried to block your course of treatment, your life-sized chess game intensified. This necessitated extending our stay in Houston from four weeks to eight. Dr. Burzynski's wife helped us break away from the negatively-charged space of our hotel suite and took us to Habitat House, where we took our respite, basking in a whimsical garden of Eden, filled with wildlife, in the middle of the city. The natural surroundings helped us all to relax, enjoy, live in the moment, and regroup.

I was extremely conscious of how much you missed your friends back in New England. Once we returned home, I was happy to be able to look out the kitchen window and watch you hang out with friends in the backyard on warm sunny days. We settled into a daily routine. Dad and I administered your cancer treatment around noon time, programming your infusions into the portable pump to be delivered through the port in your chest every four hours, around the clock. The treatment process was tedious and taxing for you. I felt this deeply. The infusions brought on a lot of fatigue, but we were all committed to the effort. We had a goal and a purpose.

Dad and I kept daily notes of your good and bad days as we watched your symptoms fluctuate and your body weaken, despite our best efforts. This was discouraging for me, but I kept my feelings to myself. I often think about my realization that your smile was fading, and it was not because you were depressed but because your face had gone numb, and the nerve pathways between your brain and your smile muscles seemed to have been pinched off. This made me so sad, yet I put on my own good face, and I kept smiling for you.

When you became too weak and unstable to navigate down the stairs to the first floor and your condition confined you to your bedroom, this was difficult to witness. A world that had been expanding for you was now becoming smaller. We looked for little ways to bring the world in. That is why I bought a variety of houseplants to bring some nature indoors and strung autumn leaves from the curtain rods with fine thread, opening the window so you could watch them flutter in the breeze.

Dad rearranged the furniture to set up a small dining area in your room, so we could all continue to sit and share dinner together. Evie brightened your space with string lights and decorated the walls with cousin Elise's fun animation art.

By late November, you had outlived the diagnosing doctors' expectations by five months, having declined the prescribed treatment of radiation. Even so, while the MRI reports indicated relative stability in the size of the tumor, your physical abilities continued to decline. Chewing and swallowing food had become more difficult. It took you longer and longer to eat your meals. I watched you gradually lose weight, muscle mass, and vitality, and along with this, you were losing your zest for life.

I remember preparing you a bowl of Thanksgiving leftovers, cutting the turkey into tiny pieces, and bringing it up to your room. That evening you told me, "I'm tired of living meal to meal." Your words made my heart crumble. Was my boy, who had held up the "NEVER GIVING UP" sign defiantly to the eye of the camera, starting to give up?

Your physical, emotional, and spiritual suffering was wearing you down. Suffering is a conscious endurance. How much more could you endure? You did not suffer alone; we all suffered alongside you, each in our own way, keeping the suffering hidden inside. Setting aside the unfinished bowl of leftovers, you were questioning whether there was any point in continuing on.

The next morning, I went into your room to check on you, called your name, and gave you a gentle shake. I said your name louder and shook you a bit more. Evie and Dad were there with me. We could not wake you up. You were in a coma. And you were so at peace. Should we have let you go then? A part of me thought we should have, but then, no. We were not ready to give you up. We disconnected you from the pump and called 911.

We spent a tense morning by your side in the ER until doctors received imaging test results. Then they whisked you away into surgery to release the cerebrospinal fluid buildup that had caused the coma. You awoke in the afternoon and found yourself lying in a Neuro Intensive Care Unit hospital bed. I was so relieved when you came to.

Ever thoughtful, you said, "Thank you" to the young orderlies (or were they interns) after they made sure you were comfortably settled into the private room. You told us: "I love you." Then your voice was gone. You could no longer discuss the medical alternatives, expound upon the meaning of life, or articulate your thoughts and opinions. You could only respond to our yes or no questions with thumbs "up" or "down."

I often reflect upon that day. Is it silly to imagine that you may have caught a glimpse of heaven and spoken with an angel who imparted that it was not yet your time? Were you meant to continue with the treatment? Or were other things you were meant to do before leaving? When you spoke the words "Thank you," it seemed you were grateful to be back, and I will treasure those words "I love you" forever.

In preparation for your return home two weeks into December, we rented a hospital bed and positioned it to face a freshly-cut Christmas tree. We had to establish new home routines since your emergency hospitalization had left you bedridden. We converted the dining room area into a private hospital ward. I stocked the dining room shelves with towels, hospital supplies, and a Pulse Oximeter while Dad suggested I stow the bulkier supplies under the bed.

There was a tangle of tubes and bags to organize and manage. Dad set up a pole behind the bed for hanging intravenous medication bags and the organic Liquid Hope tube feeding formula. Syringes, spring water, a suction pump, and hand sanitizer sat on the table next to the bed.

The hospital was sending you home to die while none of us was ready to give up. Dr. Burzynski was encouraging us to continue the clinical trial infusions because he had witnessed impossible healings over the years. *He* was still hopeful. Knowing this, you gave us a thumbs up to get back to administering the infusions. So, when the EMTs wheeled you into the house on a gurney and transferred you to the new bed, we were ready to continue the fight.

I was still clinging to hope, thinking we had a chance to turn your situation around. Dad thought so, too. I prayed the infusions could still save you. I prayed for the cancer to go away and for your brain to heal. I was doing what all DIPG parents do, praying for a miracle.

I thought the brain shunt surgery might enable higher doses of the infusions. I thought that bypassing your throat with a feeding tube placed directly into your stomach might allow me to increase your intake of calories, nutrition, and water and help you reclaim your vitality. Was this realistic? Was it denial? Was it desperation? If anything, it was Love. A mother's real, undeniable, desperate love.

Honey, forgive me for the mishaps. Programming the feeding pump was trial and error. If I gave you too much too quickly, or if your digestive tract was sluggish, everything would come up and out of your mouth. When this happened, I was afraid you would aspirate and breathe the slop into your lungs. When I saw this starting to happen, I would jump into action, wrap my arms around your torso and lean you forward to make sure your lungs stayed clear. THAT was scary! And, oh, I felt so horrible for you. Forgive me for putting you through all that. I tried my best. My best was all I could do. It was all any of us could do.

I still look back and ask myself many *What-If* questions. What if we had done this instead of that? So many what-ifs, going as far back as your August wellness checkup before freshman year. What if we had reminded you to decline that unnecessary vaccine? Did it cause the cancer in your brain?

What if we had insisted on an MRI in October? What if we had been given more time? What if we had been able to alter your diet sooner? What if we had been able to start treatment sooner when the tumor was smaller? What if the FDA had not thrown its monkey wrench into the works just as you were starting treatment? What if we could have found a local oncologist willing to commit wholeheartedly to the unconventional treatment? What if the radiologist had not delayed reporting the hydrocephalus that appeared in your mid-November MRI? What if, what if, what if. Would any of it have made a difference?"

When I sink into *What-If* thinking, I have to pull myself out of it. After all, we were navigating uncharted territory with limited information, thinking on our feet in response to each new development. Speed chess. As the battle intensified, I found myself in a constant emotional state of worry and hyper-vigilance. We brought in an experienced well-equipped team to help us.

God bless Mrs. Cuddy, our good friend who served as your visiting nurse. She pulled together a remarkable, loving, compassionate combination of medical practitioners to help us through those difficult months at home. You grew quite close to her during those last months. I am grateful to have been able to entrust her with some of the most delicate and difficult tasks of your care.

Erin, your physical therapist, showed me how to keep your circulation going by massaging your feet and legs and how to maintain your range of motion by manually rotating the joints of your ankles, knees, and hips. Pam, your home health aide, came three days a week to spend an hour assisting with your personal hygiene and bed sheet changes. Dr. Stein and her partner, Sally Davidson, graciously agreed to do house calls and neurological assessments, which were required to continue the infusions. My friends, Ann Porto and Adriene Smith, came in to support you on an energetic level with Therapeutic Touch and Reiki treatments. How could I have continued fighting without all this support?

When not coordinating visits from caregivers, friends, and extended family, I was constantly moving back and forth between the kitchen and the dining room—checking on your comfort, monitoring apparatus, and delivering water, food, supplements, and medicine through the stomach tube. Moving in a clumsy hurry one day, I managed to pinch my left thumb as the door swung shut. The bruise that grew from the base of the thumbnail took the shape of a tiny wrench squeezing a tiny heart and producing a teeny drop of blood. The bruise expressed the heart-wrenching pain deep down inside me. I never showed you that bruise. I suppressed those feelings by keeping myself busy with your care.

All I wanted to do was to stay focused on love and faith, the powers that kept you and me strong. I hope you were smiling inside as I read the many Christmas cards and letters of encouragement that arrived for you in the mail every day. I hope all the music we played for you on the stereo, over and over, did not get tedious—everything from Imagine Dragons and Bastille to Enya and classic Christmas. I hope the moments when I sat quietly next to you and held your hand truly brought you comfort.

Your present to us that final Christmas was simply your presence. While we wished for a healing miracle, it was enough to have you still with us. Then you gave us something more. Do you know what a delightful surprise it was when you gripped and brandished that old toy sword Dad had repaired for you? With that simple gesture, you were telling us, "It's not over! I still have some fight left!" But did you really? Or were you just humoring us?

On New Year's Eve, just as we were getting your treatment dose back up toward where it needed to be, you developed a breathing problem and spiked a fever. We disconnected you from the pump, called 911, and rushed you back into the hospital to be treated for pneumonia. While the orderlies settled you into a bed in the ICU at midnight, facing away from the window, I caught a glimpse of fireworks bursting over the city of Providence and could not appreciate them, not one bit. I felt completely disoriented.

A few days later, we ordered another MRI scan and reviewed the results with the hospital's leading neuro-oncologist. He showed us how the tumor had progressed since mid-November. Hospitalization had disrupted the momentum of the clinical trial infusions, which were disallowed due to hospital liability concerns. We continued to lose ground with that second hospital visit. In fact, I felt as if the ground was falling out from beneath me.

We brought you back home to give the infusions yet another try, only to return back to the hospital one more time for a stay in the Respiratory ICU to treat a second bout of pneumonia. The nurses administered more antibiotics, and we elected a tracheotomy to aid your breathing.

Do you know how hard it was for me to leave your bedside during that third stay in the hospital? I wanted to stay there every night, to sleep next to you in that lounge chair. And I would have, except family and friends insisted that I go home, get some real sleep and eat some real food.

I was so grateful to Evie, in her last semester at the university, for coming home to sit through weekend nights with you. And, I am grateful for her gem of a boyfriend, Alex, who was there to support *her* and you, and who remains at her side to this day. I was grateful for the adult friends you had in your life, mostly moms and dads, whose kids had returned to college. Some volunteered to keep vigil through the night in the hospital. They would pray at your side, regale you with old stories of mischief, or just sit quietly watching over you—guardian angels. You were never alone, my dear, sweet boy. You were always surrounded with love, and knowing that brought me comfort.

I have long reflected upon the month of February when Dad and I finally surrendered and transferred you to the Hope Hospice Care Center. I figure you had been given back to us in November to linger a bit longer and bring your life and our suffering to a meaningful conclusion.

We were given pamphlets—*Hard Choices for Loving People* and *When the Time Comes*. There was a piece titled "Giving Up, Letting Go and Letting Be" by Hank Dunn, which I found helpful. Here again, Neil, I think of that picture—you holding the "NEVER GIVING UP" sign. You were wearing the boonie hat and army dog tag, given to you by our friend Mike for good luck. Dunn's piece has one verse in particular that I know you would appreciate:

Giving up is unwillingly yielding control to forces beyond myself
Letting go is choosing to yield to forces beyond myself
Letting be acknowledges that control and choices can be illusions

There was also a valuable piece written about withdrawal:

It is normal for people who are dying to begin to withdraw, or pull away, from the world around them. This might start as early as weeks before death. They may stay in bed all day ... With withdrawal comes less of a need to talk. Touch and silence take on more meaning. People at this point may not respond to you or may look like they are in a coma. This may be their way of getting ready to let go.

Hospice meant it was time to say goodbye. Months earlier, you had told me that the hardest thing about dying would be saying goodbye. You were not worried about your own heartbreak upon leaving, but rather, you were more concerned about the heartbreak of everyone else. Especially mine, Dad's, and Evie's. You wondered *how* you would be able to say good-bye to us and to all your friends.

Well, as it turns out, you did not have to say anything. You were unable to talk, and there was no need to do so. All you had to do was listen, which was fitting because you were an especially attentive listener. Your sister and close friends had long confided in you things they would never confide to parents nor to other friends.

The two weeks in hospice were a living wake with a long line of friends. Individuals and groups of visitors came each day to say "Goodbye." They brought smiles, laughter, prayers, artwork, stories, music, flowers, photos, and mementos. Most visited with you privately while we retreated to the cafeteria space at the other end of the hallway, where we spoke with friends, family, and teachers as they arrived and lingered before departing. If I could name them all, I would fill a whole book, and what a blessed book it would be.

For example, on Valentine's day, your high school English teacher, Mrs. Izzo, brought a small book bound in burgundy cloth. On the cover, in gold lettering, was the title, Donne. It was a book of poems by John Donne (1527–1631). Your teacher had written an eloquent transcription on the title page:

To the Fachon family,

  There are no words adequate for a loss and grief this monumental. I will always remember Neil's way of looking at me sideways & smiling like he knew something the rest of us did not. I don't know if that was true then, but it certainly is now.

  Donne's Holy Sonnet "Death Be Not Proud" brings me comfort as my own family faces a terminal illness with my dear sister-in-law. It seems that Neil will also show us that Death has no right to be proud. It is not fair that he should be teaching us this. I am honored to know him & the wonderful family of which he was a part.

With love & prayers & strength,

Karen Izzo

The burgundy ribbon attached to the binding marked a page where she had written "Holy Sonnet 10." The final words of the poem, "death, thou shalt die," elicited a memory of me chasing you around the basement when you were only eighteen months old. The little you suddenly stopped in your tracks, turned to face me, and pronounced, "You have no power here!" You blew me away with a line you had just learned by watching the animation video of the Swan Princess with your sister.

The hospice staff kept urging us to discontinue tube feeding and stop providing water. We resisted a while longer as the visitors kept coming. When we finally made the decision to discontinue feeding, I was thinking back to your first breath, holding your small body in my arms for the first time and feeding you from my own breast. Holding back food and water was the most heart-wrenching decision I have ever made in my life. It meant letting go. My anguish was visceral. I felt it deep within my womb, and it was unbearable. While the nurses administered your morphine, I wished they would have given some to me.

I stepped away from your bedside, hurried down the hall to the hospice chapel room, entered, and closed the door. I sat down, alone, on the couch, and then ... I began wailing ... at God? ... to God? *Why? Why is this happening? Why did this ever have to happen?* I sobbed. My eyes and face became raw with the salt of my tears and snot. I imagined your spirit floating above me, looking down, unable to console me.

After my tears subsided, I returned to your room. Your body was barely responsive. I did sense, however, that you could still hear everything going on around you, and the visitors continued coming. On February 18, your college roommate, Stephen, came with his father to pray the Chaplet of the Divine Mercy at your side. Your high school friend, Alex G, had been coming almost every day, with his book of Psalms, to do a mitzvah with you. Your tennis teammate and classmate, Shiv, had brought you a small statue of Ganesh, the Hindu deity representing the process of death and rebirth—new beginnings. Your best friend, Andrew, wanted to leave college to come to sit with you and kept in touch by phone. My heart was deeply touched by all this sharing of love and faith.

On February 19, we received the goodbye song that your college friend, Michelle Vayngrib, had just written, played, recorded *for you,* and posted online. Her beautiful voice brought soft tears to my eyes.

> i took the train
> to a place where i could get lost
> and the people around me
>
> well they'll surround the
> body I'm wearing and
>
> i breathe in once
> breathe out slower
> you're on the ground
> i'm still floating

At that point, we were prepared to let go. However, you were still hanging on. Your heart continued at a fast, steady beat. I realized there was one more piece of business left undone. I called my own mother. Grandma was the one person from whom you still needed to hear goodbye. She had been avoiding the pain of speaking to you for months. *I* needed her to talk to you. There would be no regrets. She, you, and I all needed this closure. I held the phone to your ear, so she could speak. When she was done, I took the phone away from your ear and thanked her. Dunn, Donne, and Done.

Within the hour, Dad, Evie, and I watched you take your last breath—breathing in and then out into a slow and complete release. My heart was unexpectedly calmed. This surprised me, and then I realized why. I felt your soul had finally flown free from the cage your body had become—free from the physical and emotional suffering that we call "cancer." At that moment, I felt lighter, too. I did not know why, yet now recognize it was because I was no longer suffering from your suffering. The war was over.

We waited until Spring Break to hold your Life Celebration so that far-flung college-aged friends could attend and participate. I regret that we never discussed funeral plans with you. We lost that opportunity. So, our choices reflected our sense of what you would have liked—youth participation, inclusiveness, poignant remembrances, philosophical musings, uplifting music, positivity, good humor, social interaction, and meaning.

Neil, you once told a Boston Globe reporter, "Never underestimate the power you have to touch someone's life." Well, your time in hospice and your memorial proceedings were a measure of your life and the lives you touched. Both the funeral home and the church were packed with SO MUCH LOVE! Nearly 400 friends signed your guest book. Some of those attending may not have actually known you; however, by the time our young speakers had shared their thoughts and remembrances, everyone present had been touched by your life.

The church reception was a party. We gave it an upbeat jester theme. We decorated four large poster boards with a gallery of smiles, each photo framed in red, blue, or yellow paper—the jester colors. I threaded jingle bells with gold ribbon and sparkly "Spirit" pipe cleaners for people to take away as keepsakes. And we collected donations for your favorite cause, The Jester & Pharley Phund.

Your memorial service was the first time I had stepped into a church in a long time. And shortly after your service, Dad and I attended all the Holy Week services, Palm Sunday through Easter, there at St. Luke's Church. We turned to Jesus and his story in search of understanding and comfort. His life example, death, and resurrection brought deeper meaning to our own loss, grief, and suffering.

The month of May brought your 21st birthday, my 58th birthday,

Mother's Day, and DIPG Awareness Day—celebratory days that were difficult to celebrate without you. This time period was a bit of a black hole. All I can remember is one morning in particular when I was unable to get out of bed. You know I am usually up by 7 am. Well, waves of grief began washing over me in the early morning hours. I cried, and I cried again, intermittently. I was emotionally exhausted and distraught. At 11 am, I laid there, not wanting to face the day. Eventually, however, I dragged my sorry self out of bed.

That summer, thinking I was doing well with respect to grieving, I resumed writing monthly articles for Natural Awakenings magazine, beginning with *The Anticancer Kitchen*, sharing some of what you and I had learned together—what to eat and what to avoid. Writing about foods that prevent and fight against cancer came easily. It was a practical piece of writing, which I hoped readers would find helpful.

At this same time, I began journaling, reliving the difficult memories of your final year while they were fresh in my mind. I withdrew into this writing, spending days sitting at your computer table, capturing the sequence of events and the details, trying to rationalize it all. As I wrote, however, the reliving was causing more pain than comfort.

Maybe that is why I would wear your favorite sweatpants and gray hoodie and imagine your warm presence wrapped around me while I wrote. For comfort. To suppress the anguish deep in my heart. Occasionally, I would look out the window and find distraction in the seasonal changes of the dogwood tree, as you once did. The leaves turned burgundy and fell in the fall while birds foraged the red berries. The snow came and frosted the branches, and the squirrels nibbled on the new buds for wintertime sustenance.

Squirrel. Your power animal. This reminded me of my solitary walk around the block the day after you died. I found a dead squirrel lying on the pavement. It had taken a bad fall from high up above. It was perfectly beautiful, with just a slight trace of blood, in the back of its head, near the brain stem. I imagined the squirrel had taken a leap of fate and missed. I mourned its death with yours. It is said that when you see a dead animal on the road, the noticing is to help the spirit of the animal to move on; however, it could also be a message for the viewer.

I have read about squirrel power on a shamanic website. "Squirrel is an almighty power animal to have any time when you feel you have reached a dead end in your life or in a situation and are ready to give up. We are shown that perseverance and the readiness to try different methods are the keys to success." The notion that any obstacle can be overcome is part of the squirrel's outlook on life. There is no giving up. I can see now that this was a message for me, yet back then, I was numb and blind to it.

Neil, I mentioned numbness earlier and how it is natural for our minds to protect us from pain by inducing numbness. I have read that this can happen during the early stages of grief and that it can last a long time. Some might say numbness helps one to process what has happened at a manageable pace. I was still numb months after you died.

Eventually, though, my numbness and my self-neglect were overcome by real pain—the physical sensation of it. It crept out from my heart and moved slowly toward my left shoulder, then up my neck and down my arm, settling deep into the muscle tissue. I sought treatment for my shoulder through our family doctor, a chiropractor, and an osteopath. All of their efforts in diagnosing and treating me were ineffective. Sound familiar?

When the pink dogwood flowers were coming into bloom, you had been gone for over a year. In May, I poured myself into advocating for Brain Cancer Awareness Month and DIPG Awareness Day. I spent too much time on the DIPG Facebook pages, reading stories of other DIPG children and grieving for those families instead of tending to my grief, and this fed my inner affliction. By the end of the month, I had lost all the mobility and strength in my left arm, and my shoulder pain had become so sharp I could not sleep. Deep anguish had risen to the surface, with tears of real pain.

I pressed my osteopath to prescribe an MRI scan. The conclusion was a frozen shoulder—*adhesive capsulitis*. I was quite literally stuck and unable to move forward. Looking beyond the physical aspects of my disability, I read articles by intuitive therapists explaining that the frozen shoulder was associated with an instinctive drive to protect the heart from unbearable pain. I had been stoically holding the grief deep within, unexpressed and unprocessed.

Neil, this was the shoulder you leaned on in the middle of the night as you and I sat on the edge of your bed between infusions. Remember how we sat while you slowly worked your way through a full glass of water, so you could replenish your body's needs? Sitting up and swallowing had become more and more difficult for you. This was among my darkest, and yet most tender, memories.

At the same time, my shoulder was at the peak of pain, and my eyes started giving me problems. They had become dry and overly sensitive to light. They would squeeze shut involuntarily, and I had to will them open. This would happen while I was driving, Neil, and it scared me. Five seconds behind the wheel, without vision, could be fatal. Or, I would be walking, my eyes would close, and I would bump into the unseen and bruise myself. My eyes would squeeze shut while I was having a face-to-face conversation, and people would wonder what was wrong with me. Even in the middle of the night, my closed eyes would squeeze themselves shut even tighter, creating a tension that kept me awake. The eye doctor said my problem was old age and that I would have to live with it. It was *not* old age. My body was demanding my attention and trying to send me a message. What was it that I did not want to see?

My life without you.

I realized that the only way to alleviate my pain and disabilities was to embrace them completely and work through them on multiple levels: physical, spiritual, and emotional. This meant making self-care my number one priority. During *your* illness, I had set my own physical, social, emotional, and spiritual needs aside to focus on yours. After your death, I neglected to resume my habits of self-care.

Physically, I needed to move, stretch and strengthen my muscles. I pursued a painful physical therapy routine to work the tight knots and energy blockages out of my arms and shoulders. I joined Dad in working out at the gym, where I did core work, strength training, rebounding, and swimming. Swimming in the saltwater pool was the best therapy. The water made me feel lighter, almost weightless. It supported my heaviness—both physically and emotionally. Swimming in a saltwater pool is like bathing in a pool of therapeutic tears without having to cry them. I started with an awkward dog paddle and, after a year, recovered the strength and mobility to reclaim the grace of my breast and crawl strokes.

Spiritually, Neil, I needed a different kind of help. Aunt Sandy referred me to an energy healer and spiritual medium, Jacqulin. When I connected by phone, Jacqulin identified the part of me that had died along with you. She told me that if I wanted to move forward with my own life, I needed to resurrect that part of myself. She suggested a cord-cutting ritual. Cord-cutting sounds like I was still attached to you by an etheric umbilical cord, and maybe I was. That cord, however, was doing me no favors. It was negatively charged with loss and despair. It needed to be cut.

What was interesting is how our spiritual mother-son bond began to strengthen after the cord-cutting.

In my second session with Jacqulin, she offered herself as a channel, allowing you to speak to me through her. That was wild, huh? I often think about how you opened the session with this connective thought: "Mom, I still get the experience of this rapid acceleration of transformation in physical reality because you're here. I fulfill that karma, and you're here fulfilling that, so I simultaneously get to fulfill both." Before I could grasp the meaning of this thought, you were on to the next thought.

The intensity with which you shared your stream of consciousness held me in awe. Having much to convey, you seized this precious time and rare space with the intent of making every word and thought count. One thought flowed into the other without pause. A mind set free. And the tone, the infectious enthusiasm, was so you! It was like tuning into an astral radio frequency, and you came through, loud and clear, when I most needed you. What a gift! Thank you for that. *The rapid acceleration of transformation in the physical reality.* There we were! You gave me a lot to think about.

Then you stepped back while Jacqulin delivered my astrology reading. Born Ascendant in Capricorn with the Sun in Taurus, I was preordained to learn hopelessness. I had incarnated on Earth for the purpose of understanding the components of suffering. I was told that it was "agreed to have your son trade places with you and leave early so that you could now impart this to humanity and to the young people we're losing on the earth, who are opting out of life earlier through drugs and suicide because they lost their understanding of what they were here for ... and yet we have your son who wanted to hang onto life at all cost." This felt like a heavy lift.

The astrology reading continued by confirming my work as "a seeker in relationship with children and young people through the arts, with the capacity to affect children and their relationship to the world through the arts." That was me, to a T. I was "now being called to write and put things into motion," to find "a platform to be heard in a greater way, in such a way that will reach the many and as quickly as you can in the form of an eBook," influencing them through writing.

I felt myself being pushed forward by other words you put into my head that day, "Ya, I know, it sucks, but it's time to get on with it. You got kind of lost there and got a little bit stuck. Let me remind you who you are. You've been in the mud, I know, I've been there." Yes, you have, and yes, I was. You were also conveying that it was okay for me to use these very words with young people. They are honest, heartfelt, relational words. You had not given up. You had never given up your faith. You had found another way to continue your life mission.

That is when I resolved to write and share a collection of stories about your teen years, Neil, with the purpose of moving people's attention away from the overwhelming negative energies that have been dragging us all down. To think, believe, see, and imagine with a positive and open mindset is more important than ever before. It is this mindset that empowered me to move forward.

The process of sifting and sorting through the memorabilia, which you had accumulated in the boxes, drawers, and bookshelves of your bedroom, was like digging for buried treasure. Your favorite t-shirts, art projects, notepads, notebooks, journals, personal letters, and magic notes served to infuse my writing with your positive energy. I started reliving memories that brought a smile to my face instead of pain to my heart. I felt your presence and influence. I knew when you were looking over my shoulder and smiling about what I had written because a spiritual chill would emanate from my heart and ripple up and down my spine.

Spiritual chills have become our main way of connecting and communicating "Yes!" like the thumbs-up sign. This sensation comes from the love in your heart to the love in mine, and I thank you because it lifts me up and helps me move forward. It is also a constant calling to share my heart and help raise the vibration of our planet. My greatest hope in sharing your story is that many parents and teens will find it, read it, discuss it, and share the secrets of resilience, faith, love, and joy that you exemplified.

The physical therapy and spiritual guidance helped with my emotional healing, and I found myself on the slow, yet certain, road to reclaiming my wholeness. Healing from the loss of a child is a lifelong journey with many different pathways from which to choose. One can dwell on dark paths of denial, regret, sorrow, and hopelessness, or one can seek out the brighter paths of acceptance, joy, and helpfulness, which lead to renewed purpose. I still miss you—the physical you.

My eyes took longer to heal than my shoulder. While writing a spotlight article for the magazine, I learned about Eye Movement Desensitization and Reprocessing (EMDR), a psychotherapy approach designed to release stress associated with traumatic memories. During my first session with a compassionate therapist who has also lost a child, I bawled my eyes out. This initiated a healing response that needed more time. I am back to driving with my eyes wide open now.

Around the two-year anniversary of your death, Dad and I took a wistful walk along the beach at Rome Point, where we had once taken you on a special "rock hunt." At the low tide line, the translucent jingle shells *stood upright* (instead of laying flat) in the sand, illuminated by the morning sun. It was a magical sight to behold. And up along the high tide line, I found a wiffle ball, tarnished to a golden patina by dried algae. It looked like a large jingle bell, and I immediately thought of you. Jingle shells and jingle bells. My Dear Jester, the synchronicities made me laugh and gave me a boost.

Dad and I have continued to celebrate your spirit through involvement with organizations like the Jester & Pharley Phund, Camp Sunshine, The Tomorrow Fund, and A Wish Come True because these entities bring joy and emotional support to kids who, like you, were diagnosed with life-threatening illnesses, and to their families. If there is only so much life left to live, let us live, love, and enjoy!

The Jester Knight Comedy Night Fundraiser we hosted at the local Veteran Fireman's Club was quite the party. We felt your spiritual presence in the room. Making a special appearance in the jester costume I had made earlier that year for my return to youth work, I was in a state of pure joy.

Every time I wear that outfit, I feel my soul shine. Perhaps, I should seek opportunities to wear it more often.

When Dad and I attended a five-day bereavement session at Camp Sunshine in Maine, we got to know 37 other families who had lost children to a variety of life-threatening diseases. On the first evening, counselors taught us a song called *Hands Up*, with hand gestures and dance steps. I felt that spiritual chill. The song and dance reminded me of the energizers you taught us when you were a counselor for SLTP camp. Throughout our camp stay, uplifting fun and games helped to ease the heavy grief we all shared. Those lighter moments were when I truly felt the presence of your joyful spirit.

We had donated a Jester Smile Cart to the camp, and one volunteer told us how much it was appreciated by one boy in particular. He had been confined to his quarters due to illness and was not allowed to engage in activities with the other children. You know how this feels. When the cart, full of videos, toys, books, and games, was rolled into his room, he cried out in astonishment, "This is all for me?" I can only imagine you there in spirit when this happened. How good did *that* make you feel? It made us feel really good.

Every morning we participated in parent discussion groups, where people shared their stories and advice. Years beyond loss, many parents continue to attend camp, still feeling raw and brittle. Some Camp Sunshine parents had started foundations within a year of losing their child and were immersed in their causes. Others were still doing their best just to get from one day to the next, and that's okay. I get that! I wondered how I would feel ten years beyond your passing. It has been six years now, and I find myself at a place of acceptance, which seems like a good place to be.

The biggest takeaway from Camp Sunshine was that everyone grieves in their own way. There were separate discussion groups for young children and teens, as well as one discussion where five teens presented their insights to the parent group. The teens made the point that parents should never assume they know how their child feels; the experience of losing a sibling is different from that of losing a child. The teen consensus was that it is okay for parents to pose questions, understanding that their children will respond when and if they are ready. These five teens were all attuned to the "signs" sent their way after the losses of their siblings, and I thought that was very cool.

There were separate discussion groups for mothers and for fathers. Women tend to grieve more openly, while men tend to grieve privately. Mothers spoke of how they felt "lost." I could relate, having felt lost some days. Some mothers freely discussed how their marriages were tested by the loss of their child. Although Dad and I handle grief differently, our shared loss has brought us closer together.

So much of what we experienced with you was traumatic. Our autonomic nervous systems got scrambled, and this is especially evident at night time. When my body should be resting, it is wakeful. If I wake, as I sometimes do, at 2 am, the rest of the night can seem long to me. Dad and I are a bit like soldiers after a war, suffering our varied wounds and private emotions. I continue to try holistic healing approaches that are new to me and am experiencing good results with *homeopathy*—physical, mental, *and* emotional.

While I have written and published your *life* story, Dad is still in the arduous process of writing your *cancer* story with painstaking detail. He is incorporating documentation—emails, letters, medical records, and transcripts from video recordings. His storytelling is more expansive and ambitious in scope than mine because he wants people to know the *whole* story. You know the story better than anyone.

The federal regulatory agency's unreasonable suspension of the ANP clinical trial and its suppression of court documentation and patient rights should never have been swept under the rug. Dad's grief is entangled with anger over how the agency blocked your pathway and how it continues to exert unreasonable control over people's healthcare choices. You understand this. I remember you sitting in your hotel bed, your computer in your lap, laughing sardonically at the FDA's mission statement.

Beyond this, Dad and I have stayed in touch with Dr. Burzynski. Recently he wrote to us, "Our current results are better than ever. We are now verifying long-term survivors in our Phase 2 trials. We may have as many as 150 patients who survived from over 10 to over 35 years, not counting more in regular practice." This is heartening news! I am just sorry you are not among those survivors. Your life ended far too soon.

Still, here I am, counting my blessings and feeling grateful. I was blessed with the opportunity to serve as your mother for twenty years, knowing most other DIPG parents had only 4–6 years of life with their child. Dad and I are blessed to have been able to see the world through your life perspective. Our love for you and Evie, as well as our shared experiences as parents, continue to bind us together. And know this: never will parents love a child as much as when they have lost the child. My love grows as I go on to find new ways of expressing that love. Sharing the Jester story and your story are two ways of doing this.

I can accept that you were meant to depart, and I value the life lessons you left behind. After you discovered the Jester story in high school, you were inspired to help other young people move from hopelessness to helpfulness. You illuminated a pathway that leads from loneliness and inertia to friendship and difference-making. You showed me the power of a smile, a simple act of kindness, and an encouraging word. You engaged people in conversations and problem-solving, and you made them laugh with your spontaneous sense of humor. This was all part of your simple plan to make the world a better place. This is why I titled your story, The Difference Maker. You were a difference maker, and your humanistic story will continue to inspire others to be difference makers.

You were drawn toward the study of industrial activities that cause environmental problems and life-threatening illnesses. I often wonder what positive impact you would be having on the world if you were still here, physically. You left behind a long list of environmental issues, which you had typed out and saved to your computer just after graduating from high school. Dad found that list and printed it out. It begins with Toxins: Radioactive waste; Pesticides, herbicides, fungicides, oil; Soil contamination; Landfills. These were among the many problems you wanted to solve through Industrial Engineering and Human Behavior studies. I refer to your document to guide me in my current work. You listed many problems that worry young people today and cause many of them to feel hopeless, fearful, and stuck.

You gravitated toward these people, the ones who were troubled much like you were. And even as you wanted to understand the big picture and solve the big problems, you had the wisdom to take action in small ways—sincere eye contact, a kind word, a simple inquiry, a compassionate ear. *It looks like something is bothering you. I'm sorry. Can you tell me about it? Thank you for sharing. How can I help you?* This is how we begin to make things better—acknowledge, ask, listen, and support. It is so simple.

Like you, I have always dreamed of helping create a better world where everyone is appreciated, encouraged, included, and engaged. Two and a half years after your passing (in a rapid acceleration of transformation), I began producing the *Story Walking Radio Hour,* where I share simple ideas, actions, and choices that can bring hope and positive energy to the world. I rejoice in the spiritual chills that confirm my choices of topics, and I continue to welcome your inspiration and guidance. As I move through each day, I will keep a lookout for the divine happenstances, the "jingles" that appear along my walking path, and the difference-makers I meet along the way. The *Story Walking Radio Hour* has already accumulated over 200,000 listeners. Aligned with your spirit, I am having fun with it. We are making a difference in lots of little ways, and this brings me comfort and eases my grief.

God works through us, even in our brokenness, shining the great light of Spirit through the cracks to illuminate the greater picture. My tears come far less frequently now. They are softer, gentler, quieter, and more brief in duration. When I am feeling down, I think about you, my Jester, and call upon the enduring faith, love, and joy that reside within my own heart. And I share this with others.

Dear Neil, thank you for being with me in this life. Together, we will continue to have a positive impact. I love you to the stars and back!

Eternally yours,
Mom

CHAPTER 5

Write Out of Grief

In honor of my husband, Dr. Adam Bianchini
June 6, 1962 – August 15, 2020

By Jenell Bianchini

The journal entries in this chapter were written for my own personal use. I have chosen to present them here in their original, unedited form.

August 28, 2020

I almost broke the morning the Dr. called to tell me you weren't going to make it … I felt the gurgle of noise come up in my throat, I felt the panic and the powerlessness of the moment, and I cried out in despair. I called our precious family, I put my clothes on … then I saw a gray shadow in the doorway of our bedroom, and I ran to the shadow – to you, and I wrapped my arms around the air where the shadow had been, and I screamed to the sky "I'll love you forever," and I cried and cried. The Dr. called again 15 minutes later to tell me you had gone. I let myself wail; I don't know how long. Then I called the family. Days and days and days go by—you are still gone. I try to hold onto you, but after a few moments of seeing your face or hearing your voice in my mind, I put you away until next time, hoping I don't run out of memories or visions, or pictures or things that remind me of you. You were the greatest love of my life—you were my everything. You taught me about Jesus, you taught me how to really love, and you loved me with a fierceness I will never forget. I miss you.

My husband died on that Saturday morning, August 15th, 2020. He had been fighting the Covid-19 virus for thirty-nine days before it took his life. He was fifty-eight years old. He had a whole lot of life ahead of him, but he left a whole lot of life behind. This is my story of us.

I met my husband in 1999 when I was on top of the world. My two sons were grown, and I was thriving in my Commercial Real Estate career. I was living the life of an independent woman and looking for love in my spare time!

We met on a blind date gone wrong, as he was supposed to meet a girlfriend of mine. But she had asked me to tag along, and during that date, they didn't really connect. So when he reached out to me later to ask if I would like to meet up again, I said yes! I had recently decided to take a break from dating and concentrate on how to love being alone, but something about this man had definitely piqued my interest. His great conversational skills seemed to be almost an art form for him, and he was definitely easy on the eyes! Much later, it became clear that we were meant to find each other. This man changed my life forever!

Our first date was April Fools' Day, 1999. I got there just before him and contemplated leaving quickly if he didn't show. But sure enough, he was punctual. He sauntered over, pulled up a stool next to me, and said hi. We laughed and flirted a little bit in that uncomfortable first date sort of way, but there was an immediate chemistry between us. Then and there, our story began.

A deep connection began to form that neither of us expected, and we found ourselves smitten with each other. He was a Physician, and I was a Commercial Real Estate Broker; two professions that rarely navigated in the same social circles, but we defied the odds and became inseparable after a few months. We slowly began to blend our lives and our kids into the same world. I had two grown sons and a daughter-in-law, and he had a son who spent time with him during summers and holidays.

Before I met Adam, he had been attending a local church where he felt connected, and after a few weeks, he asked me if I would like to go to church with him. Of course, I said yes! Even though I did not have a relationship with God at that time, I was happy to go just to be near him. I had been running my own show for quite a while, truly believing I could control everything in my life, including all of the things that were out of my control. I raised my two sons alone from the time they were eight and eleven years old. During those years, I felt like I had the weight of the world on my shoulders, but God saw me, and HE just carried me then until I came to understand that concept later on. I believe HE moved us like chess pieces to get us together and, in the process, fulfill the purpose HE had for us.

We grew close over the next few months and then decided to date each other exclusively. We got engaged on Christmas Day, 2000, a year and nine months after we met. All our kids were there as we started to open presents, then Adam reached over and handed me a little black box. Now my sweet man was not overly romantic, so even though I was hoping for a ring, I had no clue when that was going to happen. I was so happy when he put that ring on my finger! I had given him my heart early on in our relationship and was ecstatic that he was ready to announce to the world that I was his and he was mine. That was the best Christmas Day of my life!

The following year, on July 28, 2001, we got married in our church with sixty people looking on. When we first met, we truly had no idea we would look back later and see God's hand in our story, but as we grew closer to God and each other, crazy things started happening! Adam came home from work one day and told me he wanted to start a bible study in our home. I wasn't sure how to even start something like that, but he did! We started with ten people, and our little bible study grew over a period of seventeen years to one hundred thirty people every Friday night. In that span of time, we went from meeting in homes, then in clubhouses, and finally into churches! Countless people were drawn to our little mission to help others, and many were impacted by our love of God and each other.

Soon people were asking us to help them with their broken relationships. We never "hung out a sign," but something we said and the way we loved each other caused others to want what we had. So we began mentoring people who were struggling with relationship issues. We never said no to anyone looking for help. Adam was always humble, though. He would tell them, "Hey, what do we know? We are both two-time marriage losers, but we'll tell you what we do now!"

While we were busy with all this, years flew by as our family grew.

Grandchildren arrived, we bought a bigger house, and we kept helping people whenever we could. The one thing that was constant in our life was that we always found time for each other. We were truly living the truth of "two become one."

In May of 2006, I was diagnosed with Stage 2 breast cancer. I had surgery, chemo, and radiation. Adam held me up through that heartbreaking time.

I knew his heart was breaking too, knowing he was powerless to stop the assault on my body, mind, and soul. Many years later, I was cleaning out a filing cabinet and came across a small plastic grocery bag. I looked inside and found the curls that he had so lovingly shaved off my head once the chemo started robbing me of my hair. I felt so loved the minute I realized what he had done … my strong, tough husband had saved my hair. He just couldn't bear to throw the curls away, knowing how much I'd lost already. Today I am sixteen years clean and grateful to God for my blessings.

Adam was responsible and never missed a day of work. He was frugal, yet he was also very generous. I was amazed at how intelligent he was and glad that he had a great sense of humor; otherwise, he would have been in "teaching mode" 24/7! He was an athlete in school, Track and Field, and Basketball team. During his college days at Brown University and then Jefferson Medical School, he pursued Power Lifting and had many Trophies to prove his skills. He worked out at the gym five days a week but still gave his time freely to someone in need. He became a National Speaker at conferences, did Talk Show Radio programs, and mentored hundreds of people! He truly was the most dynamic person I have ever known. I believe God used him so mightily because he was so willing to serve.

Adam was an Anesthesiologist by specialty, and after spending years in that field, he realized he had a huge heart for broken people. In 2009, he decided to become a Specialist in the Alcohol and Drug addiction field. He found a position as the Medical Director at a one-hundred-twenty-bed facility in our area and worked in that capacity for ten years. He oversaw the Medical Team, taught classes, and worked with the local Sheriff's Office to bring meetings to men and women who were incarcerated as a consequence of their drug and alcohol abuse. After that first facility closed, he became the Chief Medical Director at another center about thirty minutes from where we lived. He continued to work tirelessly there for five years until he died.

Adam was exposed to Covid-19 by a patient in early July 2020. When we found this out two days later, he got tested immediately, and the negative result came back the next day. Meanwhile, we had been around each other at home with minimal precautions from the day he was exposed until five days later when he came home from work with a raging fever. We then quarantined from each other, and I moved from our bedroom to the guest room.

I continued to wear a mask, take care of his meals, wipe everything down, and watch over him to the best of my ability. I took his temperature many times a day, and one day it climbed to one-hundred-three degrees. We called our doctor and asked if there was anything she could prescribe, and she said the only thing that might help was a steroid for the inflammation. He had horrible headaches and was sleeping a lot, really not caring about food as much, which was unusual for him. He felt a little better the next day, but it came back with a vengeance twenty-four hours later. During this time, I felt helpless and afraid. There was nothing I could do to turn back time and stop this nightmare … it was torture watching him struck down like this, and I was afraid I might get sick too.

At this time in July 2020, it was still the beginning of the Covid Pandemic. The protocol was not to go to the hospital but to stay home and fight it unless you were having trouble breathing. Nine days later, he woke up and told me he was having trouble moving the air around. I remember it was a Saturday morning, and there were no medical offices open, so we couldn't call our doctor again. I felt very shaky and started to tremble a little. I looked to him for what we should do next. When he told me he should probably go to the hospital, tears started to well up in my eyes because I was getting upset now, and I knew I couldn't go with him. My heart felt like it was going to jump out of my chest as I watched him gather his personal items with so much effort. The resigned look on his face was killing me … my whole world was turning upside down, and I wanted to scream.

The last time I saw my husband was July 18, 2020, as he struggled to put his shoes on at the foot of our stairs. He held his arm out to stop me when I tried to hug him … and then he walked slowly out the door with the paramedics flanking him. I watched from our front porch, just paralyzed by what was happening. They settled him into the Fire Rescue truck for the ride to the hospital.

I was moving in slow motion, wanting to believe he was going to get the help he needed, but scared to death that he might get worse. I did not think for one minute that I would never see him again. When he arrived at the ER, the doctors put an oxygen mask on him, and when he tried to call to tell me what was happening, I could hardly hear him, so we had to text each other to stay in touch.

I didn't know what to do with myself. I paced the floor, called the kids, and tried to hold on to hope, but my strength was waning. I just wanted to be with him so I could hold his hand or at least talk to him, look into his eyes, and let him know I was close.

It was during all of this upheaval that I found solace in my writing. While he fought to survive, I wrote through every emotion, furiously putting word to paper so I could get through another hour, another day. The onslaught of pain and fear would grip me, and my response was to cry out to God in prayer, in song, and in groanings that only the Holy Spirit could understand. And in those places, I found comfort … and so the gift of writing, bestowed upon me at a young age, carried me through a battle I could not navigate alone. My family and friends were close and nearby, lifting me up in prayer, checking on me, and spending time with me. Life was going on while my husband lay fighting for his life … alone except for the sounds of machines and countless medical personnel. I cannot fathom the suffering he endured while trying to breathe on his own, knowing the outcome was not looking good.

July 28, 2020

I'm praying so hard for my husband to keep fighting. He's been fighting for a week and a half to get back to just doing something as simple as breathing. Lord, please help him keep fighting, I know he's tired, please remind him of your word that is hidden deep in his heart. Surround him with your angels and with people who are caring for him, may they be compassionate and loving toward him as he struggles in that place alone without me. Lord give me strength because it's raining but I am not tired, I will keep on fighting. I'm just a little crushed and my heart is hurting for what he's going through right now. Please help us.

July 28, 2020, was our nineteenth wedding anniversary. I texted him a picture of us on our wedding day, telling him I loved him. He responded that he loved me too, but I could tell he was getting anxious, and that was something I never saw in my man. He was always so strong and sure of himself. Even in tough times, he was the one I could always lean on. Now he needed my strength, and I was going to do everything in my power to be strong for him and remind him that I was taking care of everything and everyone.

It was the hardest thing in the world not to be by his side for the last thirty days of his life. He told me he was concerned that he was still having trouble breathing, even with the oxygen mask. He stayed positive, though, and he loved telling me that all the nurses in the ICU knew I was his angel! I told him that I always knew he was mine. At this point, I was having trouble sleeping and decided to open the bedroom door and sanitize everything. Armed with a mask, cleaning supplies, and gloves, I stripped the bed and wiped down every surface. I needed to be back in our room so I could feel close to him again.

I got up early every morning and called the hospital for a report. I spoke to everyone on his case, writing down his stats and what they were doing next. Thankfully, one of my best friends was a nurse practitioner, and she would help me understand certain medical terms or procedures that I wasn't familiar with. I was fielding all the calls from his workplace as well as family and friends that were trying to call and text him. They would call me when they didn't get a response from him. I spoke to countless people every day. And we had an army of people praying for us.

Every chance he got, he would text me to say he was so worried that I would get the virus … urging me to get tested as soon as possible. I finally got an appointment and tested a week later, and the results came back negative, and we were both so relieved. By now, I had been in quarantine since July 9th' and I was so ready to get out of the house for a bit. I needed to see my family.

After two weeks in the ICU with constant oxygen dependence, they began telling him that the ventilator would be the next step. He still could not breathe on his own since he had arrived at the ER. We were texting each other throughout the day still because of the oxygen treatments. Those texts were precious because it was the only way to be close to him. He was resisting the ventilator as long as he could because, as a Physician himself, he knew the outcome would be dismal. He told me he had seen the statistics, and they were not good. So as he grew worse, I began to consider how I could reconfigure things at the house for when he came home to rehabilitate. My faith was strong, and I was sure he would be able to come back home, even if he wasn't whole. In my mind, there was no other viable option.

August 3, 2020

The days slip into each other so slowly it's almost imperceptible. I train my mind to think forward, leaving a trail of cried tears in the seconds and hours and days and weeks behind. My love lying in a hospital fighting for his life, my faith firm and strong, yet tested in the briefest moments when the pain of this truth hits me, and I scream at God.

Two days before he was put on the ventilator, we began texting all the things we wanted to say to each other … it was gut-wrenching. My strong husband kept his faith, his humor, and his love for his family at the fore-front of all we shared by text. He spoke of praying continuously for just a little breath … he said he knew God had not forgotten him and that he was a "not yetter." He knew God didn't always answer in our timing but that there was always a yes, a no, or a not yet. We talked about our family and how he didn't want to die but wanted to come home to all of us and to all the blessings God had bestowed on us. He said not to spend a lot of money on a funeral if he didn't make it and to just throw his body in the lake (we had a lake behind our house, and this was my husband's humor, meant to ease me through this, knowing he was still fighting). I told him he was the greatest love of my life, and he responded, "U mine." This is just a little bit of the hardest conversations we shared over the last two days before I could no longer communicate with him.

My heart was still holding onto him with a grip I didn't know I had. I wanted to hide from the thought he might not make it. The very next day, his kidneys started to shut down, and he had to have emergency dialysis. While he was fighting for his life, I drove to the hospital to pick up his personal belongings. I was allowed to go to the front desk, where the ICU nurses brought me his things, tied up in a sterile plastic bag. I felt like he had died already as I saw his wallet and cell phone in that plastic bag.

I went home and stood in the laundry room, staring at his belongings. I put on a mask and used tongs from the kitchen to carefully put his clothes in the washing machine. With each piece I put in, I said out loud, "you are so sweet, you are so sweet" and I just kept crying, helpless and broken and lost. I had no connection to my love anymore, except for his "things."

The next day, his doctor called to tell me that they did not have a twenty-four-hour portable dialysis machine at their hospital. They wanted to discuss transferring him to a larger hospital thirty minutes south where he could get the care he so desperately needed. He told me it was dangerous to transport him because he was on a ventilator, and they would have to get a special ambulance for the trip. I had to give them permission and audibly give my consent for his transfer and not hold the hospital or the ambulance responsible for getting him there safely. They insisted I give my verbal consent three different times to three different doctors, and I panicked at the time that it was taking.

On the day they were going to transfer him, the hospital called to tell me he was not showing any signs of life, and they said he was critical at that point. I froze inside, unable to process what they were saying for a minute. I prayed he could be moved as I waited to hear he was stable enough to make the transfer. I held onto my family and friends hour by hour. Between these minutes and hours of time passing was what was left of my life … still moving on. People were calling for updates, and I was calling the hospital four to six times a day, trying to take care of the house, pay the bills, eat, take a shower, wash my hair, want to live. My heart was so broken, and each day brought another heartbreak. It seemed there was no reprieve, no silver lining, and no rescue boat. I was running on empty and tired of fighting.

They finally moved him two days later to a facility that could handle the dialysis 24/7, but it was too late. His body had suffered so much already that his organs had started to shut down. They asked me to authorize a DO-NOT-RESUSCITATE order, and I just couldn't. I remember standing in my kitchen when the doctor asked me if I would authorize the DNR, and I immediately felt a gripping spasm, almost like paralysis, in my chest and back. I had to take a few steps before I could even breathe again. I said no that day, but several days later, I acquiesced.

I held on to hope like a drowning child, singing my songs to the Lord, praising Him all day long. By now, Adam had been hospitalized for almost thirty days. It was around this time that I began to search the filing cabinet for our wills. I was trying to remain calm, but I could sense what was coming next. My kids were calling and texting non-stop, and it was heartbreaking to hear their pleas and cries for a miracle. I would try to comfort them, but soon I had nothing to give. They sensed the emptiness that was creeping into me, and then they were the ones comforting me. My strength had now crumpled to the floor of my soul. We tried to shield the grandkids, but they were teenagers, and they knew it wasn't looking good for their Pop Pop.

My phone rang at 6 am on Saturday morning, August 15, 2020. The doctor was calling to tell me that Adam was not doing well and said, "I don't think he will be with us much longer." I cried and asked why they didn't call me sooner. He said that he was fine through the night, and his body had just started shutting down. He asked me if I wanted to come see him. I was now in shock and couldn't even find my voice. I was running around the bedroom with the phone to my ear, frantically thinking about what I should do. Then I told him that I didn't think I wanted to see him that way. The doctor said he understood and that he would call back, and that I should let the family know. But I didn't understand any of it … why, why, why? I screamed and cried as I felt so alone and helpless. I frantically looked for my clothes to put on while I called my sons. Fifteen minutes later, the doctor called back to tell me that he was gone. I felt the air go out of my lungs, and I slumped to the floor at the foot of our bed, feeling empty and devoid of life itself.

August 28, 2020
   Since you came home sick with this horrible COVID virus on July 9th,
I have not been able to write much or even really feel. I held my breath

as you got sicker, and on July 18th, when you couldn't breathe, I almost
stopped breathing too. You were sick that day and every day since you
went to the hospital. I prayed, I cried, I begged, I survived … as you lay
in there fighting for your life. I begged God to rescue you, to heal you,
to bring you home, yet you grew sicker by the day. I was on auto pilot…
praying, begging, singing, calling the nurses Doctors, checking, checking,
keeping the family and your work informed, texting you, holding on to
hope, holding on to you through that phone. Days went on and on—
you had to be moved to another hospital the week after they put you on
the ventilator, you weren't getting any better, you fought and fought and
fought … and you lost the fight here … but you gained the Glory there.

As daylight came streaming through the window, I sat on the couch
in our family room … I called it our cozy room. I sat waiting for my son
Larry to come after I called him and told him Adam had died. He just held
me for a few minutes as we both cried. My sons loved Adam like he was
their real father, and they were true brothers to Adam's son Nicholas. These
boys were beyond devastated. Nicholas was in Chicago with his mom, so
at least he would have someone to grieve with right now.

We sat in the quiet until my younger son Kyle arrived, and we held onto
each other. I think they were both holding my hands, which reminded me
of when they were young, and all we had was each other. My bond with
my sons is so strong, and I'm thankful that we can always rely on each
other. I really don't remember the words or the conversation, just that they
were there by my side, and I needed that comfort so badly. I wanted to feel
something, but it was easier not to feel at all. Our close friends soon came,
and we all huddled together in shock and sadness. The sheer magnitude
of loss felt in that room was palpable. And yet the calmness of my spirit
astounded me; I knew then that God was holding me fast.

The day was long, though I really had no concept of time because I was
just existing, feeling safe to do so with my family and friends around me.
So many thoughts swirled in my head, but I couldn't seem to hold onto
any of them. I wanted to understand all of this and think about what to do
next, but my heart begged me to be still and let my emotions reign. I fell
into a deep, dark place then, as I let the grief consume me.

As day turned to night, everyone went home, and I sat in the twilight of our house, not even turning on any lights until I got ready for bed. They all asked if I wanted someone to stay with me, but I said I would be ok … I needed to be alone that night. I knew tomorrow would come soon enough, and I would have decisions to make … tonight I would just be numb.

I went to our bedroom and sat on my side of our bed, ever so careful not to look at his side. I told my mind not to think of his suffering and him knowing that he would probably not make it. It was the hardest thing to shut off … thinking of his pain and his death, alone in that place without me. I cried until I had no more tears, then God let me sleep.

The next morning I got up early because I knew I needed to make some quick decisions regarding a final resting place for my sweet husband. I am so thankful we had prepared our wills six years before, but we never decided where we wanted to be buried. I had searched some Memorial Parks on the computer earlier that year and even showed one to Adam. I said, "Look how peaceful this one is." And he agreed. We said, let's go check it out soon, but of course, we never did.

I sat at my computer as daylight streamed in, announcing another day … I truly did not know how I could even do the next thing. All I could think was, "How can the sun come up now? How can I go on? How am I going to live without him?" I made a note of when the Memorial Park opened so I could call and make an appointment.

Then I went to make coffee, and as I looked around the kitchen, which by now would have been alive with my silly man, saying "how 'bout a cup of coffee for the husband!" I broke down as it hit me that he would never come home. He would never be in this kitchen or anywhere that I remembered him being or wanted him to be again. I cried so hard and so loud, knowing that my life had changed forever. When I finally stopped crying, I just sat on the floor in silence, reeling from the mountain of emotions that exploded in my head and my heart. I knew then that I had just broken into a million pieces. The other half of me was gone … just gone. Nothing and no one will fill that space, and the emptiness of it felt like a tornado ripping through my soul.

Much later, I called the Memorial Park and spoke with the caretaker, who agreed to see us around 10 am that morning. The Park had beautiful tree-lined roads where the branches made canopies way up high as if they were pointing to Heaven! Adam loved those kinds of trees, and I knew this was the place. I called my family, and they met me there to help with the arrangements. We toured the park and picked out a private little estate in the most beautiful spot. We all agreed it was perfect. I knew this was hard for my kids too, but they stayed strong so I could lean on them.

I followed my son and daughter-in-law to their house, which is about twenty-five minutes north of the Park, and my other son followed in his car … we were going to share some lunch together. I let them take care of me for the next two days because I was getting tired of being strong and in control. I knew I couldn't go back home yet. I would stay with my kids for a little while … I needed to be with my family.

They were so tender in their caring for me, loving me, letting me have space, and making sure I ate. Even their cats came and surrounded me, feeling my sadness. They sat at my feet or got on a chair beside me, purring and letting me know they knew. The next morning, I wrote the obituary and made an appointment at the funeral home for the arrangements. Since it was the height of the Covid Pandemic, there were no funerals being offered, just a small graveside ceremony with close family and friends.

I spent a quiet few days with my children before going home to my very empty house. It was sad and strangely haunting when I went back home … the house was missing him too. He had been in the hospital for an entire month, so the emptiness didn't hit me like a sledge hammer until the next day. Then I let myself be paralyzed by every emotion that wanted my attention. I knew there were so many things I had to attend to, but I could not even think about them. I wasn't eating much, and I didn't even care about washing my face or even taking a shower. There just didn't seem to be any purpose in any of it now. I felt like half of me died with him. I wanted to curl up in a ball and just close my eyes.

August 29, 2020

I saw the moon and the stars last night; I see the clouds and the blue sky this morning … and I wonder, where is Heaven? I want to know so I can look in that direction because you're up there now, not here with me. I miss our morning hugs, our peaceful house, our loving bond. I miss your voice, your strong embrace, your silly names for me. Your laugh, your appetite … your beautiful face. I feel lost without you. I loved our sweet life together. Yes, you were my Great love—the Greatest love of my life.

I'm afraid to write now, it scares me … I might cry again and not stop. But I can't NOT write. There is so much to say about our love, our life, our sweet story. And I'm afraid to go to bed—I don't look at your side, I pretend you are there sleeping already. Everything is still where you left it when you walked out to the fire rescue truck. I really thought you would come back … I can't believe you are gone.

My family met me at the Funeral Home to make the arrangements a couple of days later. The funeral director had asked me to bring a photo of him so he could be identified. We were not able to see him because of the Covid protocol, and I was relieved because I really did not want to see the ravages of his suffering. I brought his clothes to be buried in … not a suit for my man, like he wore to work every day, just his favorite gym pants and a beloved t-shirt. Just being in that room with my kids around me felt so strange … almost like I wasn't really there … like this was a dream I couldn't wake up from. I felt torn up inside, yet comforted by my family. They held me up in every possible way, and it gave me the strength to keep going.

August 30, 2020

21 years … it was perfect, LORD. Please forgive me, but I wanted more … more hugs, more laughs, more of this man who brought me more love, more joy, more security, more everything than any other. Our 2 become One is now just one … I'm having trouble reconciling that truth right now. My pain and loss blind me sometimes, and it's then that I don't see you, Lord, please help me go on, please don't let me feel so alone. There's no one here that loves me anymore—my husband's gone, and he's not coming back.

A week later, all the family gathered, coming from as far away as Rhode Island and Chicago. We had a beautiful service at his graveside. It was hard to watch my sons and our trusted friends carry his casket from the hearse to the grave. My legs wanted to buckle, and I wanted to close my eyes so I didn't have to see this, but I would brave this storm the same way I had braved every other loss I had ever encountered, though this one was the cruelest loss of all.

Our Pastor friend, Phil Dvorak, gave a touching eulogy sprinkled with some personal stories of working with Adam. He spoke of the many attributes my husband often shared with his patients and his co-workers. He said that Adam was never too hurried to comfort someone or to answer questions as he walked down the halls of his workplace. Adam's love for the Lord, his intelligence, his big heart, and his crazy humor were at the top of the list! Adam's son Nicholas got up and spoke. Even though it tore him apart, he spoke of how his Dad's love had been such a great example for him. Adam had been in the Air Force, and we had a military service, which included the folding of the American Flag and the playing of Taps. I had no idea how hard that salute would hit me … it was so sad, so mournful, so final. They presented me with the folded flag, and I stood very still, feeling numb and empty. The only sign of life in me at that moment were the tears falling from my face.

After the service, we went to my son's house, where we shared stories and our great love for Adam. He truly had such an impact on our family and friends, so much so that even today, many of his closest friends make an annual trek down to see me and commemorate his life.

I spent the night at my son's house, and the next day I drove home in silence, unsure of everything. All the same things were there … but he was not. Everything in every room screamed his name at me. I had put his wallet, his phone, and his car keys on the entry table by the door ... they would stay there untouched for months. I just let the darkness surround me as the day grew short, and I cried myself to sleep that night. And for so many nights after, until I lost count.

September 6, 2020

I accidentally hugged myself—and the warmth of my hands on my arms reminded me of your hug. I didn't even mean to do that, I just found my arms hugging me, and I began to cry. Then I quickly stopped … stopped hugging, stopped crying, and started writing. The pain was so deep I couldn't even process it before I stopped myself. It hurts too bad—that he's gone, he's never coming back, he will never hug me or touch me or talk to me or smile at me again.

The next day, reality set in. I had a house to run, bills to pay, all the paperwork of our finances … and the world was still reeling from the Covid shutdown … as much as I was dying inside from it too.

September 11, 2020
The pain of your absence is overwhelming. I struggle through each day, while my body continues to respond with physical pains, and my mind tries to correct everything that's not right. That task alone is insurmountable. There is no place in my mind that a life without you fits. God mercifully holds me as I try to stumble my way forward. I am thankful for my family and friends who hold me as I find my way.

———

What if I just cry? What if I let go and let it all out? Oh, I remember now …
The last time I did that I couldn't breathe, I couldn't see, I couldn't feel anything but pain; real and physical, and deep and emotional—tearing me into pieces. I had to stop wailing or die … almost acceptable.

Days turned into weeks, and I knew that I could not stay in this big house that we had so loved for nine years. It was full of beautiful memories—every room was touched by our decorating skills, and precious days and nights lived out inside these walls. It had been our sanctuary, a safe and comforting place where we disconnected from our busy lives, but one day as I sat there in our favorite spot, I looked around and knew that I could just sit there forever and pretend he was at work or a meeting and that he would be coming home soon. He would round the corner from the garage, where I always met him with open arms, and we would laugh and hug … NO! The moment that thought entered my mind was the moment I decided to sell the house.

September 23, 2020

I cried myself to sleep last night. Couldn't stop the memories, the sweet, now sad memories of my man beside me at night, holding my hand in his as we fell asleep, fingers still entwined until one of us woke and let go in the middle of the night—I'm not ready to let go love …

The Real Estate market was heating up with so many people moving to Florida, and I knew I could sell the house pretty quickly, but first, I needed to find a place for me. It was now September. Over a month had gone by. I shared my thoughts and plans with my kids and close friends, and some might have said, "You shouldn't make any big decisions for at least six months to a year," but I knew what I had to do.

Adam and I loved fast cars! He had a 1994 Viper RT10 when I met him. He said it was his gift to himself when he graduated from Medical School. That car spent most of the time in the garage, but we got it out a few times a year. It really was his showpiece … he said it was his little red head! Over our years together, we owned three corvettes; the last one was a 2020 one we ordered a year before it came in. We had fun "building" it online and waiting for it like it was our baby. Then Covid hit, and the assembly factories shut down, so the car did not arrive until October 7, 2020. Adam never got to see our baby, but I took delivery of it and kept it for five months before I sold it. Every time I drove it, I would play the music he loved and just let the wind hit me in the face while I cried. It was beautiful but just too painful to keep. And it was just like my man, though, to cover that in his last texts to me, saying, "don't be afraid to sell the new car for $$, it will be worth a lot." I felt him guiding me then and still today as I continue to live my life the way we would have if he were still here.

October 17, 2020

Your books are where you left them, your phone and wallet too, I leave them there on purpose, so when I walk by I think of you. The house is quiet and lonely, it's sad without you here, I wish you were still with me but God's plan is now so clear. You were all I ever wanted, you held me close in heart and mind and soul, and the pain is so unbearable, and the silence is so cold. One day I keep on living, the next my life's on hold.

Adam and I used to talk about "when we die" or "if I die before you," that kind of talk, and when we did, he would always say, "If I go first, don't be sad because I'll be with Jesus! Just throw me a party!" So I set about planning a celebration of life for the end of the year. I finally had something good to focus on, and I was determined to make this celebration as big and as loud as my husband had been!

We were still in the pandemic stage, and people were not gathering or traveling much, so it was no small feat to plan a sit-down dinner for a hundred people at that crazy time, but a party he would have! And at the end of 2020, ninety people showed up to honor the life and the legacy of this Extraordinary man, Adam Bianchini! We had masks and hand sanitizers at every table, a portable microphone that I sprayed between speakers, and we had music and three tables of visual vignettes that I put together to honor his life. The love in that room was visible and audible and shook the souls of everyone there.

November 15, 2020
(Written for his Celebration of Life program, held on December 30, 2020)
    Two Became One … our mission begun,
    this was the race he was destined to run
    God saw in him a warrior, an angel,
    then found a partner to soften and calm him
    And together we battled the darkness around us and God used our great
    Love as the tether that bound us
    To live as example and bear fruit for the Kingdom
    Keeping God in the middle and extending hands to the weakest
    Not saints, not perfection, we shared our own failings and
    God did the rest to bring the ultimate healing,
    To those suffering great pain in disease and depression, now saved by
    HIS love and freed from oppression.

I began to search for a new home for myself while I planned his Celebration Party. By the end of October 2020, I had a contract on a lovely Townhouse close to both of my sons. The closing date was the end of December 2020, which gave me the time I needed to prepare our big house for sale. I began to pack up nine years worth of our time in that house, including a three-car garage, and by the beginning of December, I put it on the market. Every time I showed the house to prospective buyers, my emotions were on overload. The pain of losing my other half just doubled down as I walked through each room. Flashes of the fun we had here, entertaining friends and family, and playing with the grandkids, would appear, and I could almost hear his silly laughter as I went from room to room. I became visibly upset and would even start crying. I found myself apologizing every time. Each walk-through was a reminder of how special our life was here. All the furnishings were still in place in the hope that the new buyers would want some or all of it. Our Mediterranean-style décor fit the house perfectly, but we had been talking of buying a new house and going a bit more contemporary the year before he died. So I decided to go in that direction with my new place and leave the old behind.

By the end of November 2020, I was starting to feel sad again. The pressure of getting the house ready for sale and then sorting through Adam's clothes and personal things kept the sadness and fear at the forefront of each day. I decided to take my family to our favorite vacation place the first week in December 2020. We had been going to Captiva Island since 1993, and I needed to be there again now. My son and daughter-in-law would drive us over, so all I had to do was get to their house and let them take care of the rest. That trip lifted my spirits, and from the moment we got on the road, I let myself feel free.

My grandkids were singing in the back with me, and it felt good to be alive.

The resort was decorated for Christmas and so alive with the Holiday Spirit. We had all been here a short six months ago, and it was the last vacation we had with Adam ... I could almost feel him there with us.

December 6, 2020

The sun is coming up in Captiva my love ... another day without you beside me. I hold onto each moment we shared here, and everywhere we made memories. The cool air reminds me how you loved it when the weather got cooler. I imagine this calm, this peace, surrounding you in Heaven. I hold onto you still, aching for just a bit more time with you here, but sure in the knowledge I will be with you there someday.

By the middle of December, I had a contract on our house that was set to close on March 1, 2021. This gave me the time I needed to sell the furnishings and finish packing while I slowly moved into my new place at the beginning of 2021. My sons and my friends were troopers, giving me every free minute of their time to help me pack, clean, and dispose of things. It took us two months, right up until March 1, 2021, when the house sold. I believe that having so much to do saved me from drowning in sorrow.

December 17, 2020

No, life's not fair and we were never promised a rose garden, but there's joy in the messiness of this life and there is an abundance of people who surround me and make my days easier and no, they can't replace what I've lost, but they fill me with a magnificence that is Glory to God for the difference Adam made in this world and in my life and because of that I have a deep well of hope and faith, so family and friends, thank you, I love all of you.

January 9, 2021

I'm very lonely today … there's no one I can tell it to. Everyone has their own life and things going on. I try to face all these emotions when they start overwhelming me but in the end, I'm still just left here … alone. The house is getting emptier, my heart is getting sadder and I don't know how I'll be able to live somewhere else. At this moment it feels too hard, too scary.

February 14, 2021

I have been waiting for this nightmare to be over, while I hold onto God's hand, as He whispers to me that it's ok right now to pretend.

His beautiful mind knew, and yet he never lost his faith, he never lost his humor, he never lost his love for others … he never lost because the Lord *did* rescue him, just not the rescue I wanted. But … HE rescued him nonetheless.

April 21, 2021

I don't want to write … just feel, but if I don't put it down I may explode.

I've tried to suppress it, second guess it at every turn, yet it finds me and won't leave me alone.

April 22, 2021

I have lost my compass … my love, my life. 21 years my sidekick, my partner, my angel, my warrior. I move on in silence. Most days I walk with purpose, some days I flail around like a fish out of water. Other times, I'm drowning in tears and darkness. Lord keep holding my hand, but mostly, hold my heart together as it breaks.

When thoughts would come, at any hour of any day, I would run to write them down or speak them into the notes on my phone if I was driving. Each and every word was a comfort or a pain as I poured my heart out on any page I could find.

April 25, 2021

Every step is measured
Every moment treasured
Streaming by in real time
Then floating after goodbye
"Stick with me we'll go places"
Laughing, crying, so sacred
Now to most seems hollow
Yet I know one day I'll follow
Finding joy in the love we've sown
When we finally know and we are known.

April 25, 2021

Is there poetry in Heaven? Is there even any need for words?

During the first few months after Adam died, I kept so busy that I just existed through it, but in between the lists of things that had to be done were moments where I felt lost, where time moved so slowly, and yet memories kept flying past me at warp speed. Sometimes I would be doing the most mundane, normal things, like driving, and I would literally feel like the life was just sucked right out of me—like totally winded, and I could not catch my breath. The first time it happened, I panicked and almost pulled over, but it soon passed, and I was left feeling helpless, powerless to control my own body. I had always been a very strong woman and handled many difficult situations in my life, but this unseen, unknown enemy left me with an empty, scary feeling of just being lost. I leaned on Sherri, one of my best friends who had lost her husband six years before Adam died. She understood what I was feeling even when I could barely describe it. God used her to guide me through this unknown forest where most times, I could not see the path ahead.

April 26, 2021

It's been a while
Since I managed to smile
A long long time
Since I tried to rhyme
And eons since I pursed my lips
Or even thought about a kiss
No earrings here,
No makeup there
No thoughts on hair …
Just walk ahead
Leave love behind
He was the one
The only kind
I'm living still
But my heart's now blind.

It was now early in 2021, and I found putting the finishing touches on each room in my townhouse was giving me hope for the future. Even though I went with a Contemporary design, I saved one room and made it my "cozy room." It is a library, very reminiscent of the one in our old house where I can sit and read or listen to music. It's a beautiful reminder of what had been the best twenty-one years of my life.

Around this time, I had been driving Adams' BMW. It was five years old and had over 70,000 miles on it, with the warranty expiring soon. I asked Larry to go with me to find a new car, and I settled for a slightly smaller BMW, one that was used but still had a warranty. This made sense at the time because it was white like Adams', and it had a red leather interior, which reminded me of our 2020 Corvette. The fact that I even cared about the car situation was a sign that I was starting to care about living again.

May 23, 2021

And in the quiet, I hear too much

Is there a line between grief and loss and selfishness? Grief always comes back to me … my loss, my pain, my longing to see you, hear you, touch you again. I don't know how to be happy for you—that you're with the LORD now, but sometimes I acknowledge that out loud and wait for that thought to get to my heart … I'm still waiting

May 26, 2021

I'm taking back my life today … walking with purpose, feeling my strength return, holding my head up, smelling the air the rain and feeling the pain. I hold onto you though … in my heart and mind and soul; I take you with me as I move forward, knowing you want me to. Thank you for the love, the words, the hugs, the laughs and the littlest things that only you and I shared. Those memories carry me forward, fuel my desire to keep going and never forget you were the love of my life.

July 3, 2021

There are tears waiting … just under the surface of my heart. Holding steady most days, hanging onto the edges of reality, then tilting ever so slightly to see and feel and hear the memories. It is then I cannot stop the flow and I sit very still as they roll down my cheeks, onto my hair, my lap, the floor … never finding the door to leave. They just crawl back into my heart and lay down for a nap until they hear my heart breaking again.

July 6, 2021

I'm just waiting here in the in between

Hold my hand so I know I'm seen

Touch my heart so it beats again
Hug me hard till I get to then

I can't say that any one holiday, birthday, or any other meaningful date elicited a breakdown; only sporadic moments, any day, any hour, when I would find myself ready to cry, maybe a song while driving, a memory that suddenly came out of hiding, and gratefully, there were also the memories that made me laugh and smile. Sometimes I could hear him so plainly in my mind, telling his funny jokes or calling me by his nicknames. I would smile and laugh out loud, remembering how much fun we had together. He loved the color green, and whenever I see a green straw, I remember how I would always make sure he had a green straw when I made him a protein shake or a coffee drink. I guess green straws will always be a staple in my kitchen.

August 23, 2021

I went to visit the place where we laid your sweet earthly body to rest one year ago. It was as we always wanted; a peaceful place with beautiful trees and a precious calmness. Your headstone blares out the fact that you considered "To live is Christ and to die is gain". It is who you were and what you believed. My name is there beside yours, with a hyphen between years … its up to me to continue our mission, to love God and love others. It was easier with you by my side. You were a force to be reckoned with. Thank you

Whenever I see a car like his in traffic, I think back to when he would call me after work and say, "Hey, want to meet me for dinner?" We lived so far out in the suburbs that it was faster if he drove right to the restaurant, and I would drive in to meet him there. After our dinner, we followed each other home in our respective cars, and we would pull up next to each other at the traffic lights, roll down our windows, and flirt with each other! We kept our crazy love alive, even after nineteen years of marriage!

August 26, 2021

I feel like I can live again … maybe not "I can live" but "it's ok to live" again. I have made so many things my focus since you died; I gave myself little time to live, just "do". I know it helped me, it made me breathe, it made me move, it made we walk forward … it just didn't feel like living. It's quiet now, all the focus things resolved, and its one year later. I have been sad and alone and paralyzed a bit over the last few weeks but my prayers everyday are for the healing hands of Jesus to lift me up, and HE has. I am ready LORD, I feel ready, I feel alive now, and isn't that the key to "living"?

Sometimes, when I'm in a store or a restaurant, I feel compelled to tell strangers that my husband died. Sometimes, I don't mention it at all, but going out by myself in the beginning made me feel self-conscious, and something inside me wanted the world to know that I had lost the love of my life, so look how brave I am! And some days, I'll walk by a picture of him in my house, and I'll touch his face through the glass, then other days, I'll walk by that same photo and avert my eyes because I just can't go there at that moment. Grief is strange like that … as if I could ever forget him, but sometimes I have to put the memory aside for another time.

At the end of August 2021, the whole family embarked on our yearly trek to Captiva Island! I was excited to get to our happy place again! The grandkids came separately, as they had college and jobs to get back to, but what an awesome time we had. We celebrated birthdays, fished, walked on the beach, and spent quality time just catching up. We talked about Adam and the funny things he said and did, and as we shared stories about him, we also shared in our sadness that he was gone.

September 20, 2021

I need to keep moving forward into the next thing God has for me. Days seem different … there is no anticipation of you coming home, of dinner together and sharing our day. I long for that again, even though I know its not possible. This is the lonely part, the sad part, the longing part. It's normal and needed but so painful. I keep breathing past it until I get to the next breath, the next thought, the next hour or next day. There is so much to love. I'm trying to fit somewhere but the only place to fit is right here, right now.

October 19, 2021

Rushing to nowhere to mask the loneliness
Yet each destination seems empty and pointless
My world has collapsed, I'm spinning in space
In the dark and alone, I'm left to hide in this place
Rescue me Jesus, be my light, be my hope
Hold my hand, hold my heart when I've run out of rope
Remind me again why you love me so much and shine
Your sweet love on me, lift me up, lift me up.

November 18, 2021

Grief is an assailant. It is not a sweet memory, it is not a longing for
Someone you've lost, it is a dagger meant to kill you over and over
again.

I want to be done with the grief and just move into the loss, which is
where all my sweet memories live on in my heart.

May 1, 2022

There is a danger in waking up … out of the blackness, the bleakness
The heartache, the brokenness, the fear and vulnerability, the complete and utter desolation that engulfed me when you died.

Now the air is clearing, clouds are dissipating, rain is cleansing,
thoughts are hopeful, breath is welcome, and my body is healing … but, I
feel the loneliness now, the quiet is deafening, and yet I feel alive again …
what do I do now? Now that I want to live?

All of this spills out of me like a pot of boiling water left on high too
long.

Where do I go, what do I do to turn down the heat? To just warm
up to living again? Is there some recipe to this? I'm sure there is no right
answer, yet I'm ready to move forward, recipe book or not.

July 2, 2022

It is 3 AM and I can't sleep, which is unusual for me. But I sit Here in
my house that I've grown to love over the past year. It is so Different from
the Big Italian Villa we shared … that house still holds such incredible

memories for me … with you. I move on now, not from you, just from the pain of losing you. I carry you with me always and never forget the love we shared with each other and the world. I'm going to be ok my love.

In October 2022, my sister-in-law Kathy came to Florida for a visit and mentioned a book that was written about Grief. She said Susan Lataille had compiled a group of authors for the first book and was now looking for authors for a second volume of *Shining a Light on Grief.* Kathy knows that I write about everything, and she thought I might be interested in contributing my story. I reached out to Susan and was delighted to be able to join this group. I have found that writing this chapter allowed me to review my journey with grief as a story in real-time, using my journal entries as a time stamp.

November 21, 2022

Tears like little wet fingerprints behind my eyes
Coax me back to another time
When a song comes on that says you were mine

January 25, 2023

It is now the end of January 2023 and I can say that I am in a good place physically, mentally, and spiritually. I know that nothing will ever change my love for Adam, it is engraved on me and on the world and nothing will ever change what went before or will come after. For all time he and I were the best that will ever be for me.

As I move into this year of 2023, I feel again the confident independence that I felt when Adam and I first met. The freedom to just live in the moment and work and play and laugh, as I did before. But now it's like starting again from a new perspective. The newness feels familiar, though, like an old pair of shoes that were left in the back of my closet for so long. They still fit, but now I wear them with an appreciation for what my life looks like now. I am the same person, yet different because of his imprint on me. I feel a calmness in moving forward, and I am embracing each new day and all that it brings.

I believe the key for me was to continue to seek out comfort from family and friends. I never lost my joy or my love of life, but the death of my husband caused my heart to push the pause button. I took all the time I needed to cry, to think of the past, to mourn the empty space beside me. I consider that time a blessing. No matter how hard it was for the first two years, it allowed me to make a place in my mind for all the happy memories and turn away from all the sad ones. Those two places still collide now and then when a battle ensues for prime position, so I allow it for a few minutes, sometimes longer, and then I ring the bell when I decide the round is over.

The biggest change for me this past year has been acceptance. Once the total shock wore off, the grief began to change into loss, and that was a place I could live in. The loss lets me remember him with sadness and fondness, but I'm not waiting anymore for things to get easier. I am moving on and living my life the way he would want me to … without feeling the desolation or the grief.

I meet friends for coffee and work as much or as little as I please. And I am writing, drawing, reading books again, and listening to music, all things I love to do. I like this new version of myself; actually, I love her!

And so I move on, I keep living, I keep loving … but I will never forget any of it. I move forward into whatever God has next for me, each new moment adding memories into tomorrow. I am grateful for the most incredible love we shared, but I know with great love comes great sorrow. I truly have no regrets, none at all … he was the Greatest Love of my life.

Our grief journeys are so unique, yet we meet each other there on the most human gut level. My hope is that my story will shine a glimmer of light for anyone who is battling all the dark places we must traverse when tragedy and heartbreak shatter our lives.

CHAPTER 6

God Only Gives You as Much as You Can Handle

In loving memory of the O'Leary family.

By Mary-Kate O'Leary

"Who is going to know Tommy in heaven?" That was the first question I asked Father Jim when I learned my brother passed away in the middle of the night on September 12th, 1978. I had just turned eleven years old. My brother was seven. At this time, there were four children who had this rare leukemia called American Burkitt's Lymphoma in the United States. The prognosis was not very good when he was taken to the hospital on March 28th of the same year. I remember we had those pajamas that were zipped up from your toes to your chin. My mom noticed on my brother's stomach that his veins were showing. She immediately knew something was wrong. She was a registered nurse, after all. She asked to see my chest and stomach, and I didn't have anything abnormal. The funny moment of this was my brother kept teasing me, "I saw your boobies." Well, at ten, that was not much. He was taken the next day to Worcester City Hospital and then to Boston Children's Hospital for treatment. At ten, I just knew something was wrong, really wrong, and my mom and brother were not coming home any time soon. I was so scared that something bad would happen to him. I wanted it to be me, not him. I wanted to take his pain away, but I didn't know how. Mom and Dad were so worried, and I just wanted to help.

The next five months were an absolute blur. I did not know anything. I would overhear conversations, but my parents would stop if I walked into the room. I just felt sadness all around me. My mom would stay in the hospital with Tommy, and my dad, a police officer, would work during the day and drive to Boston Children's Hospital in the evening. My two sisters would take care of us. To this day, I don't remember that my sister Karen and her husband David moved into the farm so my dad could travel back and forth and not worry about my two brothers and me living at home. I remember Tommy was in isolation due to the chemo treatment. I could only see him through a window. I hated that. I couldn't touch him or play with him, and he looked so sick. He lost all his hair which scared me. I didn't know he was that sick until I saw him through the window. For the first time, I thought maybe he wouldn't come home. Maybe I will never see him again, but I kept it all inside as I didn't want to bother anyone.

Two months later, Tommy came home to the farm. It was August. I was thrilled to have him home, but he looked very sick. We still played outside on the tractors and trucks, which he loved. We celebrated his birthday on September 4th. I did not know it would be his last birthday. One day, I found my mom praying to a small statue in my parents' bedroom. I asked her who it was, and she said it was St. Jude. She said he was the Patron Saint of lost causes. St. Jude is a symbol of choosing faith when all seems lost. She told me she prayed to him every day, and she asked him to stop my brother's pain. I told her that I also prayed. Being a good Catholic girl, I went to church every Sunday morning at 7:00 am. No music, in and out, and get your prayers in before we worked on the farm with the horses. I told her I prayed that God would allow me to switch places with my brother. "Let it be me," I said. I did not understand, but I just knew I wanted to take my family's pain away. But how does a now eleven-year-old do that?

On September 12th, I realized that it was a school day, and I was allowed to sleep in. When I woke up, my parents were at the kitchen table, and my mom told me that Tommy had passed away in the middle of the night. I would never see my brother again. I was asked to go into the living room and that was when Father Jim came to see me. Did I miss something here? Why didn't anyone tell me that the reason Tommy was home was to die on the farm? He was a fighter. He was supposed to be home for three to five days, but he survived an additional six weeks. I felt so isolated. No one would talk to me. I just tried not to get in trouble. Everyone was sad, and I just tried to stay out of the way and kept to myself. I was crying on the inside for someone to talk with me, and I was getting mad that no one was telling me what was happening. But I heard things.

Father Jim assured me that Tommy would be with plenty of people in Heaven. In fact, my Uncle Danny had passed away the month before from an unexpected heart attack. He was only in his forties. I think my mom was sad, but I didn't see a lot of emotion from her. She was just numb. How much more could someone take?

I remember borrowing clothes from the neighbor to go to this thing called a wake. There were a few things I remember vividly. First, I saw my parents cry together for the first time in my life. Second, it was an open casket, and I had difficulty staying in the same "viewing" room as my brother, but on the other hand, I was also drawn to just staring at him from afar. It was a strange feeling. I was invisible. I was happy my brother-in-law Dave sat with me. But the coffin was creepy. I did not know how to express myself, so I kept quiet. The line of people there seemed forever. The funeral home guy sat with me and said it was the longest line he had ever seen. It was because both of my parents were so respected in the community. I remember overhearing a story that my mom told people visiting. She said when my brother was in his final moments, he asked about the "stairway to heaven." How would a seven-year-old know about the stairway to heaven? I still wonder about that today.

The next day was the funeral, but my brother Tim and me were not allowed to go. I was ok with that. I felt like my mom needed space from us so she could cry, and she couldn't do that if we were around. We were to behave and give my parents a break. We fought all the time back then, but this day, we went outside and played marathon basketball. We just kept playing and playing until everyone came home. Just like a typical Irish Catholic Family in the late '70s, we barely spoke of Tommy's death, and we kept moving forward. Today, they would call this a traumatic episode, and therapy would be highly recommended to deal with grief, loss, and depression. But back then, there was a stigma if you needed to go to counseling. It was not an option.

Before I talk about how we moved on, I want to share the perspective of a child. It is unimaginable to lose someone that you gave birth to, no matter how they leave us. Through the lens of a ten-year-old, I witnessed my parents in "warrior mode." They did everything they could to help my brother AND take care of the rest of us. Our basic needs were always met. Food was always on the table. Our home was small but beautiful. No one thought or talked about emotional needs, though. That was a sign of weakness.

They had the knowledge that this ending was not going to be a good one, and they were preparing themselves for the worst. But I did not know. I couldn't prepare myself, and in fact, there were times that I acted selfishly, and to this day, I remember it like it was yesterday. My Dad and I were driving in his truck to run errands. It was right after my birthday in July, and I was excited because I got a 10-inch TV for my bedroom. In a very small house with only two TVs, I did not always get the option of picking TV shows. In the truck, my dad told me that the TV was going to go with Tommy so they could have it in the hospital. I remember being so mad that "he is getting all the attention, and no one knows I exist." My father said he was very disappointed in me. For any of you like me, you can handle someone being mad, but when they say they are disappointed … Ugh, it goes deep in your heart. If I had known what was happening, I would never have been so selfish. So, to parents, reading this book. I recommend the following:

- Counseling—Work with a counselor to find strategies to educate all family members about what is happening, as your response will have a lasting impact on everyone.
- Don't underestimate a child—We all want to "protect children from the pain," but by not sharing what is happening, you are causing pain. As a sibling, we all had different perspectives on what was going on with my brother. I think we could have helped each other out more if we had known the truth that he was not going to make it. Make sure you check in with each child/sibling to see if they are ok.
- You are not alone—I remember my mom being so strong around me even after losing her son. I wish I had the opportunity to

ask her questions about her own grief, but it was a taboo topic. We just could not go there with her. Years later, I found out that there were times when I was not around that she would have breakdowns with my aunts. I just saw my mom as a Warrior. Today, I know that strength is being able to talk about your feelings and not hold everything in. It is having the ability to ask for help when you need it. "Asking for help is a sign of strength, not weakness."

So how do you "move on" from this at eleven years old? My parents got me involved in horseback riding, which was something just for me. I loved being on a horse. I loved the smell and the strength I had when riding. I was a daredevil learning to ride and quickly participating in jumping and showing. My parents even got me a horse at home to ride. This wasn't unusual as we lived on a horse farm. The horses we had were harness racehorses. But this one was my own riding horse. It was for me. My brothers were very close. They always went hunting or fishing or played sports. I wish I was closer to them in those days. I just felt like I didn't belong or didn't know where to fit in. One good thing about the O'Leary kids was that we were strong, and we were all athletes. This was my saving grace. I suppose any of us could have turned to drugs or alcohol to get through our grief, but we channeled it into sports. My brother Mike was a great basketball and baseball player. My brother Tim played football and basketball, and I was a basketball player as well. Basketball became my obsession and my outlet.

I went to a small Catholic School in Worcester, Mass. Since I was a little girl, I always knew I would go there. My Dad would work the basketball games, and I would go with him. The Coaches would let me sit on the bench with the team. I never knew how important that meant to me until much later when I realized that those were the years right after my brother passed. It was a Division 1 basketball team, and they were the best in the State for many years. Coach Ash was the best coach, and if I wanted to go to college, I would be best with her. She never raised her voice or lost her calm. She was an incredible role model, and she pushed me hard enough that I would eventually get a scholarship to the University of Lowell in Lowell, Mass. My parents went to every game, no matter where it was in

New England. My family is known for being incredibly kind with a work ethic like no other. All of us. It has done me well … or maybe it was a defense mechanism? Either way, I graduated from College with a B.A. in Criminal Justice. I went to Anna Maria College for my M.A. in Psychology. It was my introduction to being a therapist and wanting to help others. Deep in my heart, I felt early on that if I had all the information, I could have done something differently. Maybe managed it better somehow, but the biggest impact on me was not being able to express myself. I learned to shut down and hold it in, and to this day, I struggle with expressing my true feelings. It is what I learned. I wanted to help others deal with their own trauma and learn that it was ok to express it. I was ready for this next step.

The Journey Continues

Have you ever felt you were on a journey and truly you have been in God's hands all the time? My family still never really talked about losing Tommy in 1978. I hadn't quite gotten my mind there on how difficult this must have been for my mom and dad. They just continued. My Dad buried himself in work and his horses. My Mom just never talked about it. She had beautiful grandchildren living close by and would do anything for her family. She was strong and tough as nails but loved her family. I admired her strength as a mom, but I wanted her to talk to me, not protect me. I wanted her to open up and be vulnerable so I could too. But that was an impossible task, and being vulnerable was a sign of weakness. I was experiencing highs and lows, anxiety, and insecurity. My Dad was the softy. He was so physically strong that no one would want to mess with him. But he was also one to "not make waves" and keep the peace. For someone so strong and admired, he didn't believe in himself. I got traits from both of my parents. And although people say I have an aura of confidence and strength about me, I have struggled with insecurity and self-esteem for most of my life. Haven't we all! That is normal. I look back today, and there are so many lessons learned along my grief journey. I have always been a believer that things happen for a reason. Here are a few lessons along the way:

• Therapy isn't a bad thing anymore—Trauma is real, and what we experienced was trauma. It changed our lives completely. I have learned so much through counseling. One important thing I learned is that each one of us has a different lens or view of incidents that occurred. For example, my lens of my younger brother passing away is completely different from the lens of my older sisters and brothers, as well as my parents. None are wrong. Simply different. So, what does that really mean? It means each person is entitled to their own perception of reality. For example, my nephew was very close to my brother's age when he passed away. It was very hard for my mom to be around them. She became very distant from my sister and her children. Right or wrong, my sister's family has a different view of our mom. My mom was a very tough woman. What I have learned is there is nothing harder than losing your child. How she survived this holding it all in, was a miracle. She did not have a choice. She had to take care of the rest of us and did it however she could while surviving her own grief. Seeing other children the same age as her youngest son must have been so difficult. I didn't really understand this until I dealt with it years later as an adult.

Have you ever taken a step back and tried to envision someone else's journey? What if we knew what my mom went through when she was a child? She was twelve years old when she lost her mom. She was the oldest of four, and her role in the family changed immediately. She was tough because she had to be. She didn't have a mom to teach her differently. It leads to my next lesson learned.

• Our parents did the absolute best they could—What parent is perfect … Although every parent strives for it, there is no such thing. It is so easy for us to fall into the role of judge and jury. I really try hard to "seek to understand" before making a judgment, or if I am making judgments, I catch myself and ask if I am seeing this from their perspective. I can understand and communicate better when I can slow down to see the different perspectives. I wish my mom and dad had held me more. I wish we were a little more emotional with each other. Today I am a hugger. I love hugs. My parents were not huggers. In fact, we never saw them hold hands or kiss; that was gross! But my mom didn't learn how to hug people either. No one taught her. She may not have been there on an emotional level, but she showed her own ways of loving us. Same with my dad. They truly did the best they could with minimal guidance from others. I choose to remember the great times instead of trying to understand through the eyes of my parents. They did the best they could, and that is all that matters. I accept them for who they are.

- Everyone processes grief differently—Have you ever been told, "It is time to get over it" or "You will need years to survive this loss." Quite honestly, everyone experiences grief in their own way. As an eleven-year-old, I didn't know what was happening, but I knew something was happening. I think it is important for parents to be honest with their children, but more of that will come later. There is no wrong way to process and grieve. It is about you and what you need. No one should judge your feelings because they haven't experienced your journey with the one lost. It is not a linear process. I have learned to embrace, "If you feel sad, feel it. If you feel scared, talk about it. If you just want to be depressed, be depressed; it is all ok. But getting help is highly recommended. Surround yourself with people that can support you emotionally. I have my go-to people, and what a gift they are in my life.

Re-living the Pain

- When you lose additional family members, you re-live the loss that you have experienced in your life. Unfortunately, my family has had incredible and meaningful losses in our family. We lost

both my mom and dad six months apart in 2004, my Aunt Kathy
in 2019, and then in the summer of 2022, we lost my sister Karen
and my Uncle Don days apart from each other. I feel like I have
become an expert in loss, but part of that is giving myself the
opportunity to feel whatever emotions I am having.

In 2003, my mom visited me in Florida. We had a wonderful trip, and
I had planned so much. It was a Saturday, and I had scheduled massages for
us. It was great. We were getting ready for bed, and my mom said, "May
(my nickname), you have to call an ambulance." Once again, I was clueless
that my mother was struggling. Even today, I wonder how I could not see
the signs, but here my mother was, in the midst of a medical crisis and still
solid as a rock. Indeed, she was. My Mom had a massive heart attack, and
she needed quadruple bypass surgery. I was so thankful my family took
turns coming down to help me. She stayed with me for seven weeks. I was
so scared that I would lose her. But we had some great laughs together.

One great memory I had was when my sisters came down, and we
drove my convertible on Daytona Beach, laughing and screaming. My
mother loved the ocean. It was where she found peace. It was hard to see
her go back to Massachusetts, but she returned to a beautiful new kitchen
that my dad and brothers had renovated for her. She was thrilled. I called
her every day. We had grown remarkably close. That November, I received
a call from my mom, and she told me that she had some lumps in her
lymph nodes and she was going in for tests. She called back later and
shared she had cancer, and it was bad. I wanted to get on a plane then and
there, but she told me not to and to wait until Christmas. My heart sank. I
knew she was Stage IV, and she was getting chemo and radiation.

When I came home for Christmas, I realized how sick she was. She was
in great spirits as usual, but I could see it in her deep blue eyes that she was
sad. She knew. In fact, she knew when she was in the hospital in Florida.
She chose not to share that the doctor in Florida found spots throughout her body. As an emergency room nurse for many years, she knew the
outcome. She was a smoker, and she chose not to stop. She would often
remind us it was her life, and she would live it the way she wanted.

When I arrived home, I found out that the cancer had spread to her brain, and she needed a ride to receive her radiation treatment. It was Christmas Eve, and it was one of the hardest days of my life. I was scared to take her to the hospital, but I was also happy to be there with her hoping we could connect emotionally. Let me be a shoulder to cry on. I needed that, but this wasn't the time for me; it was what SHE needed.

I was in the room when the nurse came in. My mom asked the nurse, "Did you get the results back from the test? Is the tumor getting smaller in my brain?" The nurse said, "Oh, Carol, I thought someone would have called you to let you know. No, the tumors are not getting smaller." I was speechless. I was trying to keep it together. Oh my God, my mom is going to die soon. This is really happening. I could feel the tears in my throat building like a tidal wave. I asked for a minute and left the room. I cried in the hallway and tried to pull myself together, and when I went back into the room, the nurse asked my mom if she was going to be ok. My mom said, "I will be ok if that doesn't happen again (me walking out and crying)." She did not do that to stop me from being emotional. She did that because she couldn't handle it if I got emotional. She wouldn't allow herself to feel or express what she was thinking. It reminded me of when my brother had passed. Emotional survival is an intriguing thing, and I was frustrated with it. I just wanted to hug my mom and tell her, "I am here for you, always," and she wouldn't allow me. Some would say that was selfish of her, but it was her way of survival, and I understand it now. But then, I was mad; she made me feel weak. She made me feel like speaking up for yourself was a bad thing. I needed her, and it wasn't ok to ask. I felt so alone and really couldn't talk to anyone about it. I was afraid to talk to anyone about it because I would be seen as the "weak and emotional one of the family."

My Mom and Dad were sixteen years apart in age. It was not supposed to happen this way. She had put off so many things she wanted to do, especially travel. So, it didn't surprise me that in March of 2004, four months into treatment, she told the family she was getting on a plane to see her daughter in Florida, and she wanted to put her feet in the ocean one last time. I arranged a white limo to pick her up when she and my Aunt Kathy arrived. I thought it would be great to just drive around. I had someone prepare my home to have candles lit so she would be impressed with the work I had done on my home. When she got off the plane, I was shocked at how sick she looked. She should never have been on that plane, NEVER. She loved the white limo, and when she arrived, she loved my home. She asked that I blow out all the candles so I didn't blow her up since she needed her oxygen. She still had her sense of humor.

I was lucky enough to know someone that had a home on the beach at New Smyrna. It was the penthouse, and it was just what she needed. She was in so much pain. The Percocets were not working, and she would scream in pain. I didn't know what to do, and she was so stubborn. The next day, we carried her to the beach, and she asked that she be close so her feet could be in the water. She watched me swim in the ocean, and it was amazing. Up until then, she could not sit for more than an hour without screaming in pain. But that day, she sat for almost two hours, just at peace. It was beautiful, but our moment quickly came to an end that evening. We had made it back to my home and were getting ready for bed when she started screaming in pain. I told her that we needed to call an ambulance. She knew if she went to the hospital, she would never come back. I, on the other hand, again had no clue. We had no choice but to take her. I did not want to be responsible like this. Would she ever come back? I was scared to the bones and filled with emotions. In fact, I was about to lose it in the emergency room. My aunt and I left to go take showers and change clothes. Two hours later, we came back to find my mother, MY MOTHER, crying in the E.R. No one had visited her since we had left, and she was screaming in pain and had wet herself. I asked to speak to the emergency room nurse, and I let her have it. "This is one of your own. She was an emergency room nurse, and this is how you treat her?" This poor woman didn't know what to say except I am so sorry. It wasn't her fault, but it felt good to defend my mom.

I was happy my brothers were coming down. I needed some support. My aunt went home exhausted and sad, and we were exploring options on how to get my mom back to a hospital in Worcester. Things were really turning for the worse, but she was so excited for her boys to come. We found a great company called "Angels in the Air." Our plan was to hire a private plane to take all of us home directly to Worcester, Mass, where she would be picked up by an ambulance and brought to the hospital. It was hard on all of us, but having my brothers with me was comforting. We sat together on this small plane with our mom two feet in front of us in a bed with a nurse and a doctor on each end along with two pilots. It was surreal. There was nothing to say during this time, and we each were processing our own way in silence.

My Dad was so happy to see my mom. But I think he and I were both in denial. He had moved all her furniture out of the bedroom with a special bed put in so she could come home. It was my sister Karen that told me she would not be coming home. For some reason, it was at that moment that it hit me. I couldn't be the one to tell my dad. I felt so guilty that she had come to visit me in the first place. My Dad was tired. He was scared, and I regretted not talking to him that night. He was never a big talker. But every time I left to go back home to Florida or any of the other states I lived in, he would be emotional. He cared. His birthday was coming up on April 3rd, and he was so worried she was going to die on his birthday. I told him she would never do that to him. I believed that. The next night we both stayed with my mom for the night in the hospital. My Dad slept on the floor, and I was in the chair, holding her hand. I begged her to just "let go." My sister Donna told me that my mom would never die with me present in the room. I just wanted to be with her. Later that day, I left to get my haircut, and you guessed it, my mom passed away during that time, on April 2nd, 2004.

I realized that my mom gave me a gift by visiting me in Florida. For years, I lived with regret that I took her away from our entire family during her last happy days. She may not have been able to say it, but she certainly showed her love, and I miss her and think of her every day.

My Dad was lost without her. I had returned to Florida, and he just hated being alone. He wanted me to move home so badly. I was thinking hard about it, but then I met someone that I was serious about. For years, my dad thought, "This is my last year on earth." And each year would come to pass, and we would laugh together. This year though, he had said to me, "I will die when you find someone that will take care of you." Well, that is not great motivation to stop being single.

My mom sent Les to me. He was like my dad in so many ways. He was a cowboy, and he was sixteen years older than I was. Coincidence? For the first time in a long time, I was happy. I was also unaware of things happening back on the farm in Massachusetts. My Dad was diagnosed with colon cancer. He had surgery to remove it, but I had no idea of the difficulties that took place in caring for him. My two sisters would come to the rescue whenever he needed his coloscopy bag changed, which was often. Thank goodness they were nurses. My brothers checked on my dad every day as well. I feel like I missed out by being so far away, but again, things happen for a reason. I was excited to come to the farm in November. Les had already asked me to marry him, but he wanted to ask my dad for my hand as well. Three days before we were to leave, we received a call that Dad had a stroke and that my brother Tim had found him lying in bed. Les and I immediately got the next plane to Massachusetts. I rushed to see him in the hospital. He shook Les' hand and told me, "I love you." It would be his last words to me.

Once again, I stayed with my dad holding his hand and letting him know it was ok to go. My brother Mike and I had just left the hospital. My brother Tim called and said he had passed. Another example that shows that people, or God, have control over when they leave this earth.

It was so difficult to lose one parent, but to lose both was just too much. I would like to say I dealt with my grief, but I did what I was taught to do. I buried it for years.

When You Allow Yourself to be Led to Your Destiny

Grief really does change your life. Over the next ten years, I would move across the country in search of something ... I just did not know what. We lived in Colorado, Arizona, and Kentucky, but none of those places filled my heart. There was an emptiness I wanted to fill but had no way of finding it. I found myself growing in a different direction than my husband, and we ultimately divorced. I was in stressful executive roles and was burying myself in work and not dealing with, what I now know, was grief and post-traumatic stress disorder. I literally would wake up in the middle of the night hearing my mom screaming. I missed my parents so much and realized it was time for me to go to the place that I did call home, and that was back in New England, to be closer to my family.

There were so many signs for me to return to Massachusetts. I decided to take the long way home from Kentucky and just took my time to be by myself and take the time to feel. I drove south through Tennessee and North Carolina. The Blue Grass Mountain Parkway was spectacular. I would just stop, journal, hike, and cry. I had held it in for so long that I just had to release it, and when I did, I realized I could do this. Life was changing, and I was going into the unknown. I was going to take the summer off and search for a new job in New England. I trusted my faith and gave my journey over to God. He would guide me in the direction I needed to go if I just trusted that things happen for a reason. I must say, learning to be present and to trust in God was one of the most difficult and brave things I have ever done in my life. I catch myself every day knowing that if I had taken a different road, I would never be where I am today.

I had a few different jobs when I returned. I loved being with my family, but there was still an empty hole in my heart. Does it ever get filled, I wondered. I moved to Providence, Rhode Island, and I kept noticing a job that was vacant. It was right up my alley professionally, but it was very close to home personally. It was a company called A Wish Come True, Inc. They granted wishes to children that had life-threatening illnesses. I was intrigued but not emotionally ready. I was in a job that I was bored at. I was just working to work. During this time, my aunt was diagnosed with brain cancer. I just could not believe it. I was in the room when she was told that she didn't have much time to live. I just thought, here we go again. I decided life was too short. I applied for this Executive Director position, and on her last day in the hospital, I was called to be interviewed for the job. My aunt Mary, my cousin Kara and I stayed with my aunt through her final hours. We were with her during her last breath. I have to say, watching someone in their last 72 hours is very difficult. I feel like we could do so much more to preserve the dignity of people leaving this earth. We do it with our pets. But there was some type of spiritual connection I felt. I knew my aunt would be celebrating with her family, so I felt at ease that she wasn't suffering any longer.

As for the job, I was excited for two reasons. First, as a businesswoman, I was excited that the company needed help. It had been losing funds for a long time and needed someone to take charge. I was equally excited to embrace the Mission. I quickly learned that the Mission was strong and could be stronger. A Wish Come True had people that did help the organization, but the organization was struggling financially and had lost its energy. We experienced many changes in the first two years, but the exciting part of the job was to engage with these Wish Moms and Dads. These people are warriors! Just like my mom and dad! They are grieving in a different kind of way. First, not all children pass away. In fact, in the '80s and '90s, over 60% of those receiving a wish were terminal. Today we serve many more rare diseases, but we also decided to truly be different from other wish-granting organizations. Our goal was to help families back on their feet again by providing financial, emotional, and spiritual wellness activities that allowed them to grieve the "healthy child" they once had and address the trauma that the entire family is under while treatment is occurring. All resources I wish my family could have had. I feel my personal journey has been powerful, and when I figured out I was on the journey God wanted me to be on, then life made sense. I have never been more passionate about a job than the one I am in today. My passion is to give back and help others along this emotional journey and embrace all perspectives, including those of siblings.

It has been amazing to watch the families grow and support each other. Truly, God only gives you enough that you can handle, and for me, I am so grateful and blessed that I can grow this fabulous organization. So, did I find happiness? I did. Once I loved my perfectly imperfect self, I found my soulmate David and married him. Most importantly, I had the courage to find my own soul and allowed myself to "go there." Don't be afraid of grief; embrace it. It can change your life for the good if you let the process happen. Sometimes focusing on the "why" is not the answer. I spent so many years asking, "Why me, why him, why them, why now?" Growth came when I shifted to "what now, where now, how now?" and I encourage all of you to embrace your journey wherever it may take. Today, if you are grieving, you are exactly where you are supposed to be. Allow yourself to remain open to your purpose.

With Age Comes Wisdom

In the last six months, I decided to take a chance to be part of this amazing experience of writing this book. When I committed to doing this, I had just lost my older sister Karen to a rare form of cancer. I sat by her bedside as much as I could. I was there for my family and knew talking about it was key. My sister and I had many conversations about heaven and seeing family that we missed so much. She gave me the gift of being able to talk about my feelings. I watched my family go through so many of the same emotions that I had gone through watching my mother pass. Today, I recognize that grief is truly a gift if you embrace it. It is a reminder to us that life is too short. Stay in the moment and enjoy it for what it is: your opportunity to be happy. Every day I strive for it, and I find myself more at peace. Thank you, Sista, for giving me this gift. Hug Mom and Dad and the line of so many others in heaven for me, and I will see you all soon. When my day is called, I will not be afraid. "Here I am, Lord."

CHAPTER 7

Our Playlist, Cut Short

In loving memory of Kris Ziegler Fritts.
March 9, 1971 – May 21, 2019

By Michelle Girasole

There is something about music that winds through our lives and becomes the thread that binds itself to our best memories. There is nothing like the lyrics of a special song that can transport you back in time. I have a whole playlist of songs that remind me of my best friend, Kris. When she died suddenly in May of 2019, the playlist of our lives was cut short.

My "Ziggy" playlist (her nickname) contains songs from our childhood, our formative years, and our weddings. It contains all the songs we used to enjoy together, all the songs that still remind me of her and bring her back when I am missing her most. Sometimes it is unbearable to even look at that playlist because I just don't want to revisit that old familiar ache of emptiness that arises as a reminder that she's no longer here. Other times I wistfully call it up while looking through old photos. And sometimes I listen to it as a comforting pick-me-up when I feel that empty, lonely sadness knowing I can't call her or visit her anymore. If I can't hear Kris' voice on the phone ever again, at least I can hear the music of our memories to remind me of when she was still here. And there were so many songs because there were so many years!

Childhood Songs

You see, Kris and I had done everything together since meeting in preschool at the tender young age of three. My mother retells the story of the day she dropped me off, and I stood crying, not wanting her to leave. Of course, when she came to pick me up, Mom used to say that I cried again because, this time, *I didn't* want to leave. I am certain that meeting Kris that day had something to do with it. That little, brown-eyed girl at the sandbox table turned into my best friend for the next forty-five years.

In chronologic order, our playlist starts with "*The Wheels on the Bus.*" One of my earliest memories was singing that song with Kris in a huge room filled with little kids. In elementary school, Kris and I didn't ride the bus together. She lived in the house right behind the school, and I used to love being a "walker" for the days I went to visit her after school for a play date. How we enjoyed those precious, carefree days of childhood idle time when climbing trees in the backyard was a big adventure.

Together, we joined the girl scouts, and her mom, Linda, was our troop leader. We learned many camp fire songs, but one song sticks out from these early memories, titled *"Make New Friends."* I recall singing this while holding hands in a big circle at the end of every scout meeting, then we'd squeeze hands all around the circle, and when the last little girl's hand was squeezed, the meeting was over. No doubt, all that time spent together as scouts contributed greatly to the growing bond of our friendship.

> *Make new friends, but keep the old*
> *One is silver and the other gold.*
> *A circle is round, it has no end.*
> *That's how long I'm going to be your friend.*

Friends have come in and out of my life over the years, but Kris was ALWAYS there with me. As kids, she was there to play at recess and share a ride to after-school activities in addition to scouts, we painted ceramics together and took figure skating lessons. I have pictures of us in our flamingo pink skating outfits, age seven years old, ready to skate like Bambi on ice. We had idyllic childhoods, riding bikes between our houses, playing with our dogs, and swimming at the beach or the pool with her little sister, Jen, and my little brother, Steve, who were both the same age. Life was grand with a friend like Ziggy.

In middle school, we passed notes during class, sang in the school chorus, and worked with her grandmother, who was the middle school librarian. One year, our chorus teacher asked Kris and me to shake the maracas for the Christmas song "*Feliz Navidad.*" We were so excited to have this "starring role" until the teacher announced that he decided to give the job to a girl named Danielle, who was a percussionist in the school band. (Now, I don't know if we just didn't have any rhythm, or if we were talking too much in between songs, but the job was taken away with us and we were NOT happy about it.)

Outraged, we nearly refused to participate in the concert, but our mothers would not allow the boycott. When the time came to perform, one of us had an excellent idea, but would we be brave enough to go through with it? We took our places on the risers in front of the entire audience, seated on folding chairs in the school cafeteria. When the song finally had its turn, Danielle started to shake the maracas, and our classmates started to sing:

Feliz navidad, feliz navidad,
prospero ano y felicidad.
I wanna wish you a merry Christmas!
I wanna wish you a merry Christmas.
I wanna wish you a merry Christmas,
from the bottom of my heart!

I turned to look at Kris standing next to me, and she looked at me, and the corners of her tightly sealed lips turned upwards into a smile. My lips, too, were locked shut, but I could barely hold in a laugh. If we couldn't shake those maracas, we weren't going to sing it either, and they couldn't make us! We were shaking with laughter. Our boycott of this song was a childhood rebellion that became a legend over time in our friendship. It is likely that no one but the chorus teacher ever noticed, but we knew, and I will never listen to that song again without remembering our defiant solidarity with a smile.

High School Songs

We sure had an abundance of awesome childhood memories, but our friendship didn't end there. Onwards to high school (neither of us was invited to join the choir, for some strange reason!), but we were very active all the same. We did everything we could together—school dances, athletic events, and after-school activities. Movie nights, sleepovers, trips to the mall, we did it all.

Our "playlist" expanded exponentially with all the cringy music of the 1980s big hair rock bands: Def Leppard, Bon Jovi, Poison, and ... Meat Loaf. The *Bat Out of Hell* album was a favorite—we listened to this mostly during volleyball season. We both made the team, and Meat Loaf was our team's musical choice at practices, on bus rides to games, and in the car on the way home. We could sing all the words to those cheesy songs—"Paradise by the Dashboard Light," "Two Out of Three Ain't Bad," and "I Would Do Anything For Love." Ah, the thrill of being free from parental oversight, driving through town, singing with Kris and our teammates and friends at the top of our lungs. Hearing those songs today always brings me back in an instant to our high school days. It's funny how music can do that!

Will you love me forever?
Let me sleep on it
Will you love me forever?
I couldn't take it any longer
Lord, I was crazed
And when the feeling came upon me
Like a tidal wave
I started swearing to my god and on my mother's grave
That I would love you to the end of time
I swore that I would love you to the end of time!

It sure felt in high school that *"the end of time"* would never arrive, but the senior year came all too quickly. With friends and boyfriends in tow, Kris and I celebrated our senior year with proms and college acceptance letters, high school graduation, and summer jobs. I remember feeling anxious about where we would go to college and how we would get along, being far away for the first time. While many childhood friendships end as they part ways and lose touch at this age, I got to bring my BFF with me to college. Both of us chose to attend the University of Rhode Island, and of course, we HAD to live together.

College Song Collection

As roommates, we did it all together, from the freshman orientation weekend to dorm move-in day, to all-nighter study sessions to keg parties and spring break trips. Kris was always the life of the party at URI, and barely a day went by for four years that we didn't eat together, study together, walk together, and have fun together. We really did it all, right by one another's side.

We'd enjoy football and basketball games, where we learned and joined the crowds in chanting the Rams' Fight Song:

We're Rhode Island born
We're Rhode Island bred
And when we die
We'll be Rhode Island dead.

So, go, go! Rhode Island, Island,
Go, go! Rhode Island,
Go, Rhode Island,
U-R-I!

If there wasn't a sporting event, we'd go to clubs to shake off the week's studies and dance the weekends away. Our favorite was the Bon Vue Inn, a weather-worn, grey-shingled building right on the ocean. Upstairs Bon Vue hosted live bands, and in the basement, there was a dance floor and a DJ. One song that always got us out on the dance floor was "Dancing Queen" by ABBA. I mean, what girl can resist twirling around to that classic?

You can dance,
You can jive!
Having the time of your lives.

Oooh, see that girl.
Watch that scene.
Digging the dancing queen!

We sure enjoyed college life together. She was such a huge part of my life. The night I met Rich, my future husband, at a dorm party, she was there to throw me "that look" across the room when he started flirting with me. The night he picked me up for our first date, she was there to help me pick out the perfect outfit. She was the first friend I called when we got engaged. In fact, she already knew he had bought the ring a few weeks earlier and kept it a secret! Kris soon became one of Rich's favorite people, too. Her friendship was woven into the daily fabric of our lives. We belonged to each other.

As girlfriends do, we planned and enjoyed vacations, barbecues, bridal showers, bachelorette parties, weddings, and baby showers. Of course, we jumped for joy when we learned we were pregnant at the same time. We gave birth to our boys just eleven days apart. It was a very special time in our lives.

Sadly, in our 20s, our lives got very busy with work and family life. It was also then that life took a hard turn for Kris. She was diagnosed with non-Hodgkins Lymphoma at age twenty-six. I rushed over to her mother's house when she called to tell me the awful news and listened with hidden horror to the discoveries of her tumor and details of the treatments she would have to endure. I knew that my job was to encourage her through it. I was devastated for her as she shared fears of undergoing radiation and losing her hair, but I assured her she would beat this disease. And that is just what she did. She never gave up.

As a proud cancer survivor, Kris became an avid fundraiser for Dana Farber, Jimmy Fund, and the American Cancer Society. We were all so grateful for the caregivers and the research that saved her life. We figure Kris and her "Team Tigger," made up of her family and her many friends, raised over $100,000 through the years. (Her team mascot was Tigger, symbolizing her bouncing back from the disease. She eventually beat it three times!) The cancer community became part of her life and ours.

There are many angels that work in the cancer industry for sure.

The oncologists, nurses, and hospital workers fight this battle every day. Research has come leaps and bounds in saving lives. However, the treatment can be toxic. The cure for Kris' first cancer—the radiation treatment that killed the lymphoma cells—caused the second cancer a few years later, a carcinoma on her tongue.

She endured more surgery and radiation to get rid of that, struggling to heal while caring for her toddler son, Cameron, and her new baby girl, Kacey, who was just nine months old. It was her pure love for them and her desire to live to be their mom that made her endure the torturous treatments. When she beat it again, we knew she could do anything!

Unfortunately, we were not able to live close to each other. Kris married a policeman from Wellesley, Massachusetts, who had to live close to work outside of Boston. Rich and I chose to live near the beach and bought a house in southern Rhode Island. It was an hour and half drive to visit, and I regret the long spans of time that went by without seeing each other. Many days, I felt a longing to spend a lazy, carefree day of our youth together again, and I battled feelings of regret by calling often and sending frequent text messages to maintain our close connection.

When someone you love has had a life-threatening illness, you know that time is precious and time together is not guaranteed. We did our best to get together, despite the distance, and enjoyed watching our children get to know each other.

Our kids grew fast, and we always made an effort to gather for an annual Christmas brunch with all our high school girlfriends and all of their kids. (For the record, we never played "Feliz Navidad" at those parties!) That brunch was a tradition we all loved and continued, especially when Kris divorced, and her cancer returned a third time. Yes, it came back again.

We all wondered, "How much suffering can one woman take?" In the last half of her life, Kris expanded my understanding of the answer to that question. Cancer is hell on earth. Her parents and sister took her to endless doctor appointments and visits to Boston hospitals for treatments. Hospitals are not places to go to get rest, and I will always marvel at the extraordinary effort it took her and her family to fight that disease three times. But they did it!

Kris beat the odds and survived the radiation of the tumor that had wrapped itself around the main artery that runs to her brain. Although a third round of radiation was more than the doctors would normally advise, the risk of damaging that artery during a surgical removal could cause brain damage, so she took her chances on more radiation. Enduring that treatment was mentally and physically exhausting, but our brave cancer warrior did it! She wanted to live, and so she did.

She got the news of her third remission as we were approaching our 40th birthday, and we all decided we were not going to let this milestone pass without a big celebration.

Six of our girlfriends decided to take a four-day cruise to the Bahamas. Kris was still recovering from the treatment and was having trouble swallowing. It made me nervous that something was lurking below the surface of her health recovery that we didn't know about.

We noticed she'd cough a little when she was eating, but there, on the deck of the cruise ship, she made a toast with fruity cocktails as we raised our glasses and celebrated four decades of friendship. For a few days, at least, we set our fears and worries aside and embraced the opportunity to escape the harsh reality that Kris had been facing.

By day, we lounged on deck chairs by the pool, laughing at stories and catching up on our jobs, homes, parents, husbands, and kids. You would have thought no one else was on board except the steel drum band and us.

Life was good! Our friend had beat cancer for good, and we cherished the time away from our hectic lives. On the last day, an island stop, we relaxed fully. The troubles of the world were literally an ocean away as we lounged in hammocks and sipped rum drinks under the swaying palm trees. The smiles on our tanned faces reflected the contentment we all felt with each other. We wished the trip would never end.

Back in Boston, there would be more trouble ahead. That pesky coughing Kris was dealing with was investigated by her care team, and it was determined that the radiation had damaged the tubes in her neck, and food was getting into her lungs. She would be subject to pneumonia, and they decided her eating was too risky. She would have to use a port for nutrition. Kris would never again be able to eat food.

No more eating food?! Good Lord, how deflating this news was for her. Every time she shared a new diagnosis, we would be bewildered by the unfairness of it. I remember feeling guilty that I could enjoy my food while she had to take in a brown liquid through a port on her side. I worried that the solution she was being fed was not enough nutrition to sustain her forever. The foreboding reality of her not being able to do a basic human function like chewing and swallowing food was a sign that her life was so fragile and her situation was permanent. This was not going to end well, and it broke my heart.

How many more challenges would she endure to stay alive? We had no clue how she did it. But she just kept on doing the next thing she had to do to stay alive to spend more time here on earth with her precious kids. Her parents helped her sell the house and move into a condo closer to them, so they would not have to drive so far to help her. The kids were so active in school and their activities, as we had been at their age. Cam and Kacey were such good caretakers for their mom, but she needed her parents nearby.

That cut the distance between us in half, and we were able to visit more often. I began expanding my business into Massachusetts, so I could have an excuse to visit her more often! I took on business projects in the field of cancer prevention, inspired by everything Kris had gone through.

Her throat had been exposed to so much radiation it became fragile. Her care team in Boston were superheroes to all of us, as were her sister and parents, who advocated for her continued daily care. It was soon determined that her vocal cords had also been damaged, and consequently, she lost her voice.

That one hit hard for all of us, as phone calls were a lifeline for our connection to Kris. Not only would she never sing our favorite songs again, but she could no longer speak to us in full voice. I remember being very selfishly angry about this loss. This disease had stolen my best friend's voice, and it felt like one step away from taking her away from me altogether! Picking up the phone and calling my BFF to chit-chat was a basic function that we had enjoyed our entire lives. Hearing her voice was how I could tell if she was "up" or "down." She had the ability to make me laugh or cry with that voice. Calling to talk was no longer an option! This devastating loss took away our phone conversations and made visits very difficult. We wanted to talk endlessly, but it was physically hard for her to do that now. Again, I felt guilty and angry that I took for granted abilities that she no longer had.

In typical Kris fashion, she adjusted. She learned to speak in a whisper. She never lost her sense of humor and joked that now that she couldn't yell at the kids, she'd be an even better mom. Imagine!

We'd get group texts from her, Linda, and Jen, as the hospital visits seemed to bring endless bad news. She had resisted for so long, but it was next determined she'd need a tracheotomy to continue breathing. She didn't want the kids to be frightened by it, nor did she want to be connected to machinery to breathe, but when it became inevitable, she just took it on as the next battle she had to fight in her health journey. I marvel at her superhuman perseverance. She must have grieved every loss of function that happened to her body, but she never gave up. Kris was bound and determined that life would go on. And, so it did, for years.

After she lost her voice, we switched over to texting. Thank God for technology, for we shared pictures and "talked" about all the things that adult girlfriends do, sometimes football or baseball or work, but mostly the kids, their activities, milestones, or fun "remember when" memories from our shared past.

I called her "my second brain" because, for me, she was the one who remembered everything, all the details from an entire lifetime! I'd call on her memory when mine would fail me.

"Hey, remember that girl we met on the quad when URI had that festival? I saw her the other day and could NOT remember her name …"

"Zig, what was that movie we watched that time we were in NH, the one with that actor who …"

"What was the name of that song we skated to at Mount St. Charles when we wore those flamingo pink skating outfits? …"

She always knew, even the trivial things. She knew everything about my life because she had been there for most of it. Kris' friendship had been my "comfort blanket" my whole life. Her body was failing, but her brain was sharp as ever.

Her 'voice' always came through in the words she texted. She had this amazing positive spirit, with a curiosity for the present, a warm recollection of the past, and ALWAYS a bright hope for the future. She inspired me to be the same way.

Yeah, Kris was THAT friend. I wish everyone could have a best friend like her. More like a sister, joined at heart. I cherished our friendship, and she knew it.

On her forty-eighth birthday on March 9th, I brought my new puppy to meet her and delivered a special gift of four dozen roses—one for each year of her life. It was a crazy gift, and she shook her head in wonderment as I brought the bouquets through the front door while trying to manage a hyper dog on a leash. She'd often laugh at the stupidity of things that I did, and I could see in the sparkle of her eyes that she was amused by the whole scene. She was happy Scooter, and I were there, but a deep tiredness behind the smile indicated she wasn't feeling well, so we kept the visit short. I drove home in tears, remembering the young, vibrant girl Kris used to be, compared to the battered body she was living in now. Her suffering has robbed her of the celebrations that make life special. It was so hard to see her like that because I knew our lives would never be the same again. I knew that day she would not be with us forever.

But as I left, I had no way of knowing it would be the last birthday we celebrated together or the last time I would ever visit her. I always thought she'd just keep fighting the next health battle and win. Had I known, it would have been impossible to leave. It's better that fate doesn't show its hand, I suppose, but we never got to say goodbye. I don't think my heart could bear it.

It's hard to talk about the way she passed. I think I have blocked the details her mother shared with me about it. The radiation had done its job of killing the cancer, but it also caused more damage to her upper body than she could survive. Kris had gone in for another surgery on May 21, 2019, and it was there on the operating table that she finally lost the fight for her life. It happened so fast, but it had also been happening for years. Still, her last breath took our breath away! After so many life-threatening hurdles and so many death-defying comebacks, we had honestly begun to believe her death was not an option. We knew how hard she fought to live, and so it was hard to believe—even after all her health struggles—that she was really gone.

I'll never forget standing in my living room, checking my phone for texts, and seeing one from her sister to our group chat. Those were usually requests for prayers that Kris would get through another health challenge. They were not usually good news, but I remember reading Jen's somber words that she had passed. It felt like a punch in the gut. Instantly, the blood drained from my face, and I had to sit down. What? No! I read it again. I could not breathe or speak. No! I did not want this to be happening. My heart was instantly and permanently broken, for the loss of my best friend, for her children who lost their mother, and for her sister and parents, who had been through so much with her to prevent this from happening. But it was happening. Kris was gone. I cried deeply until I could not breathe from the core of my being. I had lost a very, very special part of me when Kris left this earth. We all had.

Funerals and Goodbye Lyrics

How does one survive the grief of a loss so great? I had always found comfort in the rituals of wakes and funerals, but not this time. This time, it was my best friend. She had died too young, at the age of forty-eight, and I wasn't ready to say goodbye. Whoever is ready to end such a precious friendship?

Kris' sister Jen had asked me to choose a poem to read after she had given the eulogy. She and her parents wanted me to pick a reading that reflected Kris' strength and courage, as she had fought the good fight against cancer three times in the course of her life. I found a poem called "Brave Warrior," which won their approval. I wanted to read it with the strength Kris had exhibited while battling her health challenges, so I must have read it out loud a hundred times at home to make sure I would not break down and cry in front of everyone attending her funeral.

I had no doubt the bitter emotions of grief and loss would be strong going back to Kris' church to say one final goodbye, but I was resolved not to "lose it" reading that poem. Her young kids and her parents had been through so much already, and all of us wanted to celebrate Kris' life and love that day. I had to stay strong for them, as she had.

However, I had not been very strong the night before at the wake. Kris had brought joy to so many lives, and we all were in mourning. Rather than being comforted by the presence of old friends and loved ones, I personally felt the grief of each person that entered the building. Kris was our hero, our inspiration. She had been for years. And now she was gone. The overwhelming finality of her loss was no longer something that might happen someday. I could not breathe, and tears welled up in my eyes as I looked into the eyes of each person who was feeling the same way I did. This was not fair! This should not have happened to someone like Kris! She fought too hard to stay here on earth, and it was not okay that her life was cut so short! That damned disease stole our precious friend, daughter, and mother, as it had so many before her.

I cried when I saw her high school crush walk in wearing a Tigger tie, a special nod to her favorite mascot. I cried at the sight of our dear friend from college, just staring dully at the photo slideshow of Kris' smiling face through the years, taking it all in with a crushing sadness that sent me out of the building to compose myself. My emotions were out of control—I wanted so badly to be the smiling, cheerful reminder of how special she was, how strong she was, but I was not strong. I was overcome with grief in her absence—she was my closest friend in the world, and it felt like half of my heart had been ripped out. I would never be whole again because she was gone.

Most of the night, there was a lump in my throat that threatened the words of comfort I was supposed to share with others. I was on the verge of tears the whole night. I was weaker than I ever had been because part of me was now missing. I could not contain this grief that was not mine alone. It belonged to everyone who knew and loved her.

The next day, at the funeral at her family's church, the love was palpable. I sat in the second pew with Rich. We were the first to arrive. I planned ahead because I knew I would need some extra time to compose myself before her family arrived. With good reason, I had been crying a lot in the last week. The hot and salty tears came easily ever since getting that sudden tragic text from her sister. I could not fathom life without her. And yet here we were, at her funeral!

The last time I had been in this church was on Kris' wedding day. I blinked back the emotional tears as she said her wedding vows, as she had done for me. Her wedding song, "From This Moment On" by Shania Twain, flashed through my thoughts.

Strange side note, I do not recall any of the music that played at the funeral—I think my brain latched memories onto the songs of joy and perhaps released from memory the songs related to pain and grief. That said, any traditional funeral music, such as "Ave Maria" or "On Eagle's Wings," can send the tears flowing each time I hear them, bringing me back to church funerals for loved ones throughout the passage of time.

Her family had now arrived at the church, and as I watched her parents, Linda and Chip, enter the sanctuary, the sadness in their eyes caused an instant lump in my throat. No one should have to bury a child, and they had been through so much over the last two decades. As her beloved children walked in, now teenagers aged fifteen and thirteen, they warmed my heart with their sweet faces. I decided at that moment that I was not going to cry reading Kris' poem if it was the last thing I ever did for her. I wanted this poem to inspire her loved ones, not cause them more sadness. She would have wanted that, too.

A Message from an Angel

I remember turning from the kids to compose myself and looking up beyond the urn at the beautiful stained glass window behind the altar as the organist began to play. I had grown up in Christian churches, and most of them displayed a cross or a stained glass window of Jesus behind the altar. But this window was not of Jesus at all.

This particular window depicted an angel pointing down, at some women in mourning, just like me. This scene was of Easter morning, and those women were Jesus' loved ones—maybe his mother, Mary, or his friend, Mary Magdelene—and the angel outside the tomb. It was the perfect vision for a funeral. Strangely, I had not noticed that at her wedding.

Suspecting this image might be a "sign" of some relevant message, I quickly flipped through the Bible to read the details of that Easter story to know what that angel said to those women outside the tomb. I read the words the angel had told them, *"Do not be afraid, you are seeking Jesus, but he is not here among the dead."* They had feared his body had been stolen but learned from the angel that he was alive.

The message I took away from that verse at the time was that Kris was not here in the golden box that contained her ashes. She was alive in spirit! My faith helped me to see that, like Jesus, she was still with us to this day, alive in our hearts and in our memories. She always will be. That was just the message I needed. It was heaven-sent. She was with us right now! That realization was so comforting at that moment and still is.

Brave Warrior

I took a deep breath and let it out slowly. The service began, and each reading and song brought comfort to all of us who loved her. I was able to get through that reading, drawing on the strength of the brave warrior I was honoring, my bestie, Kris. Faith has a way of giving us strength, enough to be brave warriors fighting off the grief we all feel when we lose someone we love. The poem I read ended with these words.

We know you'll continue to watch over us
For it's something you've always done
And that you'll never be too far from us
In the days and years to come

So Kris, sweet dreams for now …
Peacefully may you rest …
Confident in all the hearts you touched
And in all the lives you blessed

We do not doubt we'll see you again
Someday whole and completely healed
For Zig … you were one of the bravest warriors
To ever grace life's battlefield!

I'm not going to lie. The grief of her loss still hits me like a ton of bricks. Usually in small, unexpected moments. Like the time that summer when I took the kids for ice cream across the street from the Bon Vue Inn. I looked up from my ice cream cone, saw the old familiar building, thought of Kris and our good times dancing in there, and just burst into those old familiar tears.

On my own forty-eighth birthday, a few months later, grief washed over me when the first few birthday greetings started rolling in from special people, and it dawned on me she would not be texting me her cheerful birthday love. We always celebrated with each other. I had to simply look up to the sky and know she was there, smiling down. I let my imagination wonder what she'd say and chuckled to myself that she'd likely delight in teasing, "Now, you're always going to be older than me!" She would have been right. She'll stay forever young, as the song goes. If you don't laugh, you'll cry.

Writing this chapter, I had to keep an entire box of tissues next to the computer. The memories mean that the love we shared is still tucked away in our hearts and always will be. I may never stop feeling the hot sting of tears in my eyes when I miss her and the friendship we shared.

I still feel a deep emptiness in the wake of the death of my best friend. My whole being wishes Kris could just walk in the room so we could reconnect and pick up our special friendship where we left off. Perhaps that is why I go to visit her gravesite, to reconnect with her spirit, where her physical remains lie, to spend some time reliving the memories, having a "conversation" with her there. Perhaps that is why I created her playlist— the songs that keep her memory alive.

Now, I see Kris in her children. It brings me joy to see her in their features. Her son has her eyes, and her daughter's smile is always a throwback to Kris at her age. Just this past weekend, our boys went off to their college freshman year. I sent Cam a UMass sweatshirt for his graduation and texted him when he left for the campus to wish him good luck. He responded with Kris' bright enthusiasm.

His sister Kacey is following in her mom's footsteps, playing volleyball, and was excited that I wanted to come see her play a varsity game. I'll sit in the bleachers with her mother's spirit, I'm sure, and "remember when" we were Kacey's age, blocking side by side at the net in a high school game.

Life goes on, and we have all learned to live with the grief of the loss of someone so dear. I also think that experiencing the deep grief of loss helps you deal with the smaller "little griefs" that life hands you. For example, this week, I am dealing with the flood of emotions of becoming an empty nester, mourning the end of a phase of motherhood that I cherished. My children are no longer living in my house, and the details of their days are no longer mine to coordinate, as they had been for two decades. The reminders around the house that they are no longer here are everywhere! Even though I know I can pick up the phone, hear their voices, and visit them again soon, the family unit is forever changed. The "empty nest" is real. The pain of loss is similar, and I have learned to "allow it," to sit with it, to let it wash over me in waves, and then to breathe it out, to let it go. You literally hold grief in your lungs, and you can breathe it out.

Singing is one great way to do that.

Oh, and donuts help.

I kid you not! Seriously, on the afternoon we learned that Kris had passed away, I was curled up on the couch sobbing, and a colleague of mine had happened to call. When I explained what had happened, he shared some advice he had gotten from a friend when his own dear friend had passed away suddenly.

He said, "You know, Michelle, in time, you'll get through all the stages of grief, but it is rough right now. Do you know how a friend of mine advised me to deal with grief? By eating sugary pastries. It helps! Go get some Allie's Donuts, and don't worry about the calories. You'll feel better …" It was good advice, and I offer it to you now. Yes, there's always a sugary pastry nearby to make you feel better, but we know that is not a healthy long-term coping strategy, is it?

Life goes on. Grief goes on, too. Be gentle with yourself as you experience it. If possible, I try to take a few moments to let the sadness wash over me, cry it out, and breathe through it. I look at the photo of us smiling together at Disney so long ago. I may wear a necklace she gave me for a couple of days. The emotions are real, and it is best not to ignore them.

Music really helps. Make a playlist dedicated to your loved one. Dance and sing and remember and cry and laugh. Know this—your loved one forever lives on in your heart and memory, always. And the songs are everlasting.

Kris' spirit is everlasting. I will always be so grateful for her light, laughter, and love. I will always be grateful for the songs that make our lifetime of special memories come alive. I can't help but shake my head in frustration that our playlist should have been longer. Our life together should have continued on through many more special events that unfold through time. We should have had more days spent doing the things lifetime best friends do, with music marking many occasions. The special songs that mark the special times in the future won't be our shared times—our children's weddings, the vacations we won't get to take, the anniversary parties Kris won't be at, two grey-haired ladies exchanging photos of grandchildren, etc. Those future memory songs will go on someone else's playlist, and so there is a natural sad wistfulness that we won't make those memories together. But, as they say, the show must go on. Life must go on with the living.

As a result of experiencing this deep felt loss of Kris' precious friendship, I no longer take the people I love for granted. I am more reserved with my time because I know time with loved ones is not infinite. I stay connected to the friends we shared because they also remember and share those memories. While our relationship cannot be replaced, I try to be a good friend to others, as she was to me, paying it forward, almost as a tribute to my Ziggy.

I will end this chapter with the lyrics of a song that came to me only recently, perfect for this occasion. Over the past summer, I discovered and started enjoying the music of a band called Tedeschi Trucks. This particular song is titled "Soul's Sweet Song," written for their beloved band member and friend who passed away. It is a message of loving reminder and hope in each rising sun. I hope you find it online and maybe even add it to your playlist! It definitely has a home on my Ziggy playlist forever.

Soul's Sweet Song

After the tears and the spate of lonely days,
After the noon-born shadows slowly fade,
After your heavy stone was rolled away,
Rollin', rollin',
That's when it finally came to me.

Now there's no use wishin' for your sweet return
'Cause I see you in the mornin' sun
And I hear you on the whispering wind
And I feel your rhythm movin' me
'Cause your soul's sweet song's still singin'!

CHAPTER 8

Blake's Story — From Grief to Gratitude

A mother's memory of and relationship with her only son.

By Elizabeth Phinney

I was three months shy of my 36th birthday and about to have my first baby. I started the pregnancy at a svelte one-hundred-thirty-eight pounds (I'm 5'8"), thin enough to fit into my mother's wedding gown. And there I was, seven months later, about to give birth at a whopping two hundred ten pounds. What had happened to me? Don't believe it when they say you will lose weight after the baby because this little guy didn't take that extra seventy pounds with him when he left his cozy womb.

But Blake made up for it in absolute perfection. The weight gain concern slowly dissipated as this little bundle of pure love entered my life. He had a small bit of reddish hair—from my grandmother's side—and a magnetic charm that was alluring and adorable. It was clear early on that he was very smart (everyone thinks that of their babies, but he really was!). He caught onto things very quickly and certainly loved to make sure that we saw that, so he proved it over and over again.

When he was just ten weeks old, I left him for ten days. There was a business conference in London at which my attendance was required. I was completely naïve as to the ramifications of this departure. (Sidebar: We have come a long way since 1988 in recognizing the psychological damage that happens to kids zero–eight years old when certain events occur—like the disappearance of your mother at ten weeks old.) Unfortunately, that was just the first trauma that this little boy had to endure before he was eight years old.

Let's back up just a bit to give you the picture of the family that this child of innocence was born into. Both his parents were career professionals. His father was the owner of the largest and most successful motor coach charter company in all of Boston. His mother—that's me—was the owner of a million-dollar destination management company that did all ground services for incentive and corporate groups that visited Boston—from sightseeing tours and special events to hospitality and theme parties. The day Blake was born was in the middle of the tenth round of a twenty-group back-to-back (one group leaves the same day the next group arrives) program. Each group had 1,200 people. I was running all the ground activities while Dad ran the motorcoach company that transported all those folks around from the airport to the hotel to the tours ... you get the picture. And, to top it off, the bookkeeper I had hired to keep all the groups separate and the records straight was doing a horrific job, so I had to fire her right before the baby was born. Henceforth, I had to do all the bookkeeping. In a nutshell, Blake was born into a chaotic environment. Consequently, we had a nanny lined up who began when he was just one month old.

Soon our lives got into a routine. When work was over, Dad would take over with Blake, and I would do the kitchen routine of dinner and dishes. Though Blake slept through the night before I went to London, that was not so much the case after I got home. This smart little boy wanted to make sure his momma was always there, so every night, around 2:00–3:00 am, he would start to cry. I would go up to his room and coddle him and sing to him and rock him back to sleep. Some nights it took ten minutes, but most nights, it took almost an hour. I know you are supposed to let them cry it out, but I didn't have the heart—a first baby and working mom's guilt kind of thing.

Just twenty months after Blake's birth, our first daughter was born. He was primed to be a big brother! He entertained his baby sister and played with her whenever he could. Fast forward another thirty months, and baby sister #2 was born. Not to be overwhelmed by this responsibility, he took on the challenge and realized he could be a playmate to both of them, and from experience, he had the baby thing down.

Unfortunately, life around him was anything but blissful. Without going into the gory details, his dad's business failed, and he ended up as a salesman for one of his previous competitors. I sold my business so I could stay home with the children. My husband and I had a successful joint venture which lasted about a year. But our arguments and fights were now twofold. Life at home was not a happy one. So at 4½, Blake, his two sisters, and I moved in with my parents, seventy-five miles away from his dad.

His dad had been his best buddy. They were together from the minute Dad got home from work till the minute he went to bed every day. Losing him and only getting to see him for a weekend every other week truly broke his heart. He was very sad and angry. But the days turned into weeks which turned into months, and he got adjusted to the new life in the small country town by the sea.

Just a few weeks into kindergarten, it was easily apparent that this little boy was very smart (I know I said that before, but now the teacher agrees) and needed constant stimulation to keep from getting into trouble. So, reward charts were set up for him based on his behavior to help the teachers make it through a class without him causing too much chaos. The hardest part was that because he was so smart, and I must add, charming and polite, he could argue (or charm) his way out of any situation or wrongdoing. He was a challenge to everyone but also a dear, sweet boy who simply missed his old life.

We left my parents after nine months and moved into another home. Blake was now the only male in the house—a role he took very seriously. I had no idea he thought of himself as "the man of the house" until I started dating, eventually marrying a man. At first, everything was fine, and everyone got along great with my new husband. It was then that Blake came to me with the proof of his dilemma: "But, Mom. I thought that I was the man of the house. Why did you marry him? We don't need him." I was dumbstruck! I had no idea. No matter how I tried to explain, there really was no explanation that did not sound selfish. Not only had I taken him away from his dad, but now I took away his sense of self-importance. And, to top it off, his stepfather was not nice to him and very emotionally abusive (completely kept hidden from me). More trauma for this little boy, now almost eleven years old.

It took a year of suffering until Blake decided he wanted to go live with his dad. At twelve, he is legally allowed to make that decision, so that is what he did. By this time, his dad had started another business and was once again doing quite well. His dream had come true to have his "buddy" back. Unfortunately, things don't always turn out the way we think they will.

The town that Blake had just come from was an all-white community of 3,500 people, with one boy from the Philippines in his school. That was the extent of diversity. He moved into a city of approximately 30,000 people: over 50% Hispanic, a large percentage Asian, and only 11% white. He was in for a rude awakening. Being the new kid, he was bullied, kicked, and even had his food spit on in the cafeteria. But, as time went on and his wit and charm supported his survival, he was able to gather a great group of friends from all nationalities and walks of life. That experience strengthened him and taught him how to befriend those from other cultures and embrace their differences. It gave Blake a sense of integrity and honesty. He was growing up.

By ninth grade, however, things with his dad were not working out so well. As I mentioned, Blake was not a "normal" kid. School was very difficult for him as he did not learn the way he was being taught. He would get frustrated and angry with lots of things. Unfortunately, his dad needed him to be "normal." He could handle "normal." So, when Blake was not "normal," trouble ensued. The tension mounted until finally, in April of his freshman year, Blake swallowed a bottle of his anti-anxiety medication. I will never forget the phone call.

I was grocery shopping and in the produce department when my phone rang. It was Blake. He was crying. He was scared. He was panicked, "Mom, I took a bottle of pills, and Dad won't take me to the emergency room." I repeated back to him what he had told me to make sure I got it right, and he said yes. (For a multitude of reasons, when emergencies like this come up, I go into calm. Needless to say, my calm demeanor in this situation was helpful.) I asked when he did this. He said it had been about ten minutes. I figured we had maybe a half hour before this stuff would start to get into his system, and I was about an hour and a half away. I asked to speak with his dad. His father's response was startling, "He'll be fine. He's just doing this for attention. He doesn't need to go to the hospital. If we do that, I won't get home till 2:00 or 3:00 in the morning, and I have work tomorrow. He'll be fine."

Remaining calm, I hung up and called Blake's therapist and told him what happened—thank goodness he picked up the phone. He immediately called Blake's father and warned him that if he didn't take Blake to the hospital, he could be found guilty of negligence and have Blake taken away from him. Blake went to the hospital.

The next morning, I called the house around 8:30, figuring that Blake would still be in bed, and I wanted to see how he was doing. I was shocked to learn that his father had sent him to school at the regular time. His response: "He's not going to pull that stuff and think he's gonna miss school!" So, I called the school and spoke to Blake's guidance counselor. Another savior to Blake—every morning of school, when he had a study hall during the first period, this amazing woman would let him come into her office and rant for 45 minutes about his dad and everything he was miserable about. She would calmly listen. She obviously cared deeply for him and only wanted to support him.

I asked her if she had seen Blake yet that morning, and she said that it was not a study hall day. I told her what had happened, and she promised to find him. She then informed me of "the protocol," which now had to take place based on the school's guidelines regarding what to do with what they considered a suicide attempt. Blake had to be evaluated by a psychiatrist and was sent to a children's psychiatric hospital for two weeks for observation. As the pill ingestion was more of an attention-getting episode than an actual suicide attempt, he was released. The fortunate part was that because of this event, the school then put him on an IEP—Individualized Education Program—for the duration of his tenure in the town's school system.

What else came from this episode was that Blake's father *was* put on probation due to negligence, so a social worker was now assigned to Blake. They met once a week for months. Actually, he was a really good guy, and Blake liked him a lot. I think he gave a good deal of support to Blake in this trying time.

Later on, in the summer, Blake and some friends were trespassing in an abandoned building in the city. They were chased by police, and Blake got caught and arrested. He was released with no further actions taken, but his dad told him that if the social worker found out, they would take him away from him and put him into the foster care system. I did not think that that would actually happen but I deliberated for a good twenty-four hours of painful soul-searching to do the right thing for Blake. What was going to be the best thing for him? If the social worker knew, it would help him support Blake all the more. I just didn't believe that his dad would lose custody. Because of what his father implied to him, Blake told me that if I told the social worker, he would never speak to me again. I made the impossible decision to inform the social worker, and my son kept his word.

School started up again with Blake now in his sophomore year. Blake's father had bought a vacation condo in New Hampshire where he would take the kids on weekends, which he had done the previous weekend. One of Blake's pastimes was to whittle with a knife and stick. He kept the switchblade in his pants pocket. When he returned to school the following week, the school thought he had been smoking outside, so they searched his pants for cigarettes. Instead, they found the switchblade. School rules were very clear—weapons in school led to immediate expulsion. But Blake was on an IEP, which meant that the town was now responsible for his education. He was taken out of the high school and put in an evaluation school for about six weeks, then into another one for another six weeks. From there, he was placed in a residential school for troubled kids, where he stayed until November of his junior year.

At this point, he was not speaking to either his father or me, so his adult cousin stepped in to help negotiate his release. He had been visiting Blake while he was at the residential facility as he knew Blake was having a hard time, and his father and I were not able to help. In the meeting with the committee of people who convened to decide Blake's fate, I insisted that Blake not be allowed to go back to his father's. I knew that Blake did not want to come back to my home, so Cousin kindly stepped in and became the parent. One thing he mandated, though, was that Blake and I would have to go to therapy and reconnect. It had been eight months since he had spoken directly to me. I was heavily involved with all the school decisions and drove up for every meeting, but Blake would not enter the room until I left it.

Finally, in the spring of his sophomore year, while he was still in the residential facility, Cousin would pick him up, and we would all meet for therapy, including the cousin's mom, myself, Blake, and his dad (who only lasted 2–3 sessions). We met at least every other week, as I recall, and within several months, Blake and I were in our own therapy. I remember sitting on the couch, and he was on the chair across the room. He still wouldn't look at me but would speak to me through the therapist. Slowly but surely, week after week, he would finally face me and speak directly to me. We got it all out. He wanted me to know how angry he was, and I wanted him to know how sorry I was. With months of work and determination on both our parts, we figured it all out, and by the fall, when he got out of the residential facility, we were into Sunday afternoon visits every other week and kept that schedule until he went to college.

Cousin relocated so Blake could live near his dad's town for school. It was now the fall of his junior year, and the town had its own special school for special kids, and that is where Blake went. Cousin mandated that he get a job, which he did, selling shoes at a nearby strip mall. There were quite a few rules that Cousin required, but as long as Blake didn't want to live with his dad or with me, he learned to cope. Cousin and I took full custody of Blake that spring.

When it was time for his senior year, all agreed that he was ready to go back to regular public school for that last year. After all, Blake did want to go to college, so he had to start getting some grades on his transcript. He went to the local high school, walking 2 miles each way as he did not like school buses, then went to his job after school and on weekends. The job got more interesting when he switched to working at the local video game store—much more fun for him.

His high school senior year, dare I say, was "normal." Things worked out well enough with Cousin, though by graduation, they were both ready to call it quits. Remember I told you my boy was smart? Seeing as his senior grades were really all that were used for his college applications, he was on the Honor Roll the entire year and got accepted at the University of Massachusetts main campus in Amherst, beginning the following January. Proud Mom, for sure!

Cousin and I happily drove him to Amherst that January and helped him move into his *single* room—the benefits of being on an IEP and need-ing special consideration. His dorm was in the freshman area, his window overlooking the woods behind the building. That first evening around midnight, he got a knock at his door. It was a woman who happened to see his profile in the window of her old dorm room. His "mohawk" hair-style was intriguing (remember, we are talking 2008.) That night started a wonderful friendship that blossomed into something more after about six months. I will call her "B."

Blake's college life was pretty ordinary in that it included classes and homework, as well as drinking and smoking. He did get a job at the local video store and pretty much settled into life in western Massachusetts. That summer after his freshman year, he lived with some buddies in a house west of Boston, working and partying as all twenty-year-olds do. Back to college in September, he was frustrated by never being able to sign up for courses he was actually interested in, but rather having to settle with what was available that was still part of his Liberal Arts curriculum. He was not happy with the limited options and the huge class sizes, but he made the best of it. He was happy with the friends he made (there were quite a few of them), and they all hung out and partied together. He kept his studies up but knew that after that spring, he wanted to take a semester off. He spent the summer in Boston with his Boston friends, and in the fall, he went back out to Amherst but took a break from classes. He moved into a house with four or five other students, B being his roommate. He had just celebrated his twenty-first birthday.

It was a Saturday evening, and the house was having a party. Blake and his buddy J decided to go get some more beer at the liquor store just half a mile down the road. It was around 10:30 at night. They jumped on their bikes. On the ride home, each of them carrying an 18-pack of Pabst Blue Ribbon, Blake was riding on the outside in the bike lane. He was struck from behind by a car. The mirror of the car broke off, so it is guessed that the mirror hit Blake from behind, sending him flying in the air, landing on his head, breaking his neck, and killing him almost instantly. J was thrown onto the grass, breaking his leg.

The chaos that followed is unimaginable for this cadre of "kids," some in their late teens but mostly early twenties. Especially B. She had just received her EMT certification the day before and sensed a heartbeat, so she tried to give Blake CPR to no avail. She was twenty-one years old, trying to save her love's life. I cannot even begin to know what she went through that night, but she was and always will be one of the bravest people I know.

It was 2:30 in the morning, and my youngest daughter was at my bed-side waking me up: "Mom, C's on the phone and is hysterical. She won't tell me what's going on." I woke up with a start and grabbed the phone, only to hear my oldest daughter emotionally out of control on the other end. As mentioned before, in times like this, I go into calm.

"Mom, he's dead! He's dead! Blake's dead!"

"Honey, you have to breathe. Come on, take a breath. Now you said he's dead. Who's dead, sweetie?"

"Blake, Mom! Blake is dead!"

"Okay, sweetie, now breathe. You say Blake is dead?"

"Yes, Mom. Blake is dead."

"Okay, honey. You have to calm down and tell me what happened."

There are so many different ways I should have handled the next few hours, but, needless to say, there had been no rehearsal for this event, and I was completely taken aback by the news as well as the hysteria of my daughter, who was in her sophomore dorm room over two hundred miles away.

The fact that I was learning this information from my child vs. my ex-husband was an entirely different conversation. He had been called by the Amherst police department. He tried to call me, but I had no phone in my bedroom, and my cell phone was downstairs, so I did not hear it ring. Why he didn't then call my younger daughter, who lived with me, to have her wake me up is beyond comprehension. To actually call our other daughter, wake her up, tell her the news, and then say, "You have to call your mother and tell her." Can you imagine being nineteen years old and having to call your mother in the middle of the night to tell her that her son had been killed? To this day, I will never understand what he was thinking.

Stupidly, I walked my younger daughter back to her bedroom and left her there to deal with this alone—what was *I* thinking? My "calm" mind had to figure out what I was going to do in the morning. Why I didn't just cuddle up with this dazed and fraught sixteen-year-old haunts me to this day.

Apparently, in her "alone-ness," she posted Blake's death on Facebook.

As a result of that posting, at 7:30 in the morning, my three best friends were at my doorstep, ready to take charge and guide me as to what to do. A good thing since I was numb, a zombie. Per their instructions, I showered and got dressed. Two of their daughters were coming over to stay with my daughter and keep her company—fortunately, they had all been friends since they were little girls. The four of us climbed in the car for the two-and-a-half-hour drive to Amherst.

The entire day is mostly a blur, but I will share what I do remember. It seemed like each of my friends took on a role of support. There was JL, who drove and was definitely in charge; JT, who took on the friend role and ended up calling everyone that needed to be notified during our ride; then there was P, who took on the role of "mom." She sat behind me in the car, and every time I started to cry, she would reach from behind and rub my shoulders to console me.

After a good hour of driving, it started. I had heard and read about it and studied it in my religion courses in college. I understood what it was for and what it meant, but I had certainly never experienced it. I began to wail. It was this unholy sound—a scream that came from the depths of my belly. Each wail was guttural and loud and only ended when I ran out of breath. I felt exhausted at the end of each cry, but I needed to do it again and again—like I was trying to purge something from deep in my soul. The void was growing, taking over my body. The pain was excruciating, unspeakable. For the next twenty minutes, I just sobbed and wailed, feeling emptier and emptier.

P undid her seat belt so she could really hug me from behind, and JT leaned forward and was gently rubbing my leg. JL just kept driving, wanting to get us to Amherst as soon as possible.

When the car pulled into the driveway, B came running out to meet me and gave me this amazing hug as we stood there and sobbed in each other's arms.

Up to this point, she and I had only met a few times. I had been out to Amherst a couple of times, and she had been to my house with Blake a couple of times. Their most recent visit, coincidentally, had been the previous weekend. He hated where I lived because it was the place he had to go when he was taken away from his dad so many years previously. But somehow, he and B showed up that weekend to spend the day. We had lunch on the deck and went swimming at the beach. It took a bit of convincing to get his little sister to join us, but she did—thank goodness, in her hindsight. We took pictures, unfortunately, none of him and me nor of him and his sis. Hugs and goodbyes till the next time. Smiling and waving, I was happy and grateful for their surprise visit. Little did we know that it would be the last. In hindsight, it was his "goodbye."

JL, JT, P, and I joined the others on the patio as we all sat in disbelief at what had happened less than 24 hours before. These were his friends, his core group that cried and smoked and sat in stunned confusion. They ranged in age from eighteen to twenty-four. They didn't know how to process what had happened. We adults in the room took on the job of helping to console these kids. I suppose it was my way of avoiding dealing with my own despair. Cousin and his mom showed up and wanted to see the body. JL, ever the leader, made it happen. I could not—it would be far too overwhelming to have to remember him that way. The previous weekend gave me the picture of Blake that I needed to focus on.

We walked down the street to where the accident happened. I sat on the curb next to P. I knew it was the right spot because you could see the stain of blood on the road from his head trauma. I sat and stared and sobbed and sobbed and sobbed as P kept her arm around me and let me sob into her bosom—a very vivid memory for me. I am pretty sure that this was when it struck me that he was actually gone. Seeing the site of his death and being in that presence, I had an overwhelming sense of loss and grief, a heartache, unlike anything I had ever felt before. I couldn't imagine that this hollowness and desperate loss was something that I had to face every hour, every day, for the rest of my life. So, I cried and cried until my sobs got shorter, and there was nothing left. I just couldn't cry anymore.

The only other memory I really have of that day was what happened on the car ride home. At some point, I began to laugh long enough for the other three to be concerned. When I stopped, I said, "This is a parent's worst nightmare … and I am living it!" Then I put my hand to my mouth, gasped, then whispered, "I didn't know I was going to have to be this strong." At that moment, I knew that there was more to come in my life for which I would have to be strong.

Blake was not a religious kid, so we had a service for him at the local community center. Friends of mine from far and wide came—I have no idea how some of them even heard about it. Blake's gang from Amherst and Boston came, and I must admit, my heart broke for each and every one of them. They were all still kids, basically. Not much of a reservoir of experience from which to gather the strength to handle this kind of event. They did the best they could as one after another got up onto the stage and said what they wanted to say. Blake was actually a musician in a "screamer" band (he was the screamer!), and one of his music buddies had written a song and played it. Blake's father actually tried to say a few words, with our daughters by his side, to help get him through it. There was no way I would even try. I was numb, just going through the motions. Everyone was pretty much in a daze as the day passed on. Just let me get through today … the week … the month … the rest of my life.

About six weeks after Blake died, his friends in Amherst held the first Blakefest. Older daughter C, a few of her friends, Cousin, and I attended. What a gift it was to get to know his friends a little more and spend some more time with them. Their love for Blake was very evident, and their need to keep him alive in their hearts was all around. To keep that going, each year around his birthday, we would hold a weekend Blakefest at our house. His friends returned year after year for almost ten years. For me, I was so grateful for this connection to Blake through his friends and overjoyed that he had known their love. For some, however, it got to be too much. It just made them sad to return each year, so Blakefest kind of fizzled out. That made me sad, as staying connected to them was staying connected to him. But it was during the last Blakefest, when we all told of our gratitude for the year, that I had a confession to make. Coping with the loss of my son was the bravest and most difficult thing I had ever done. It had made me stronger than I ever knew I could be. As a result, there was nothing left that could happen in my life that would beat me. If I could handle this, I could handle anything.

The year following Blake's death is pretty much a blur. I functioned and got my work done. Managed to do my workouts but did fall back on some unhealthy binge eating, specifically, "not-giving-a-shit" eating. I ended up gaining about ten pounds. I was living with my mom and helping her as much as I could. My younger daughter was also with us, still going to school each day. I think it's safe to say we all just went through the motions of daily living. My poor mom had a birthday just three weeks after Blake died. I will never forget her sitting in her chair, looking at me with tears streaming down her face, "It's just not fair. Here I am turning eighty-seven, and he barely made it past twenty-one."

About a year later, I was sitting at my desk in my office when Blake's voice, clear as a bell, came to me over my right shoulder, "Mom, you've had your year. It's time to get out there again." And then he was gone. I was confused about how to respond to his admonition, but I finally started listening to online seminars and webinars and learning from all sorts of gurus. One that struck me with an intriguing message and energy was Brendan Bouchard. He was involved in the creation of the Expert Industry Association, which was launching its first convention. I had been working as a Certified Personal Trainer for eleven years and had become an expert in the field of fitness after forty-five, so I thought attending this convention would be a great way to "get out there again." So, I signed up. That was the beginning of a 2½ year educational journey, attending eleven more conferences and nurturing the seeds of my future life.

One of those conferences was in Las Vegas. West of Vegas is Red Rock Canyon, which is great for hiking. A couple of friends from the group and I decided to do just that and left the lights and sounds of the city to venture out into nature. Fortunately, both of these women were of the same spiritual mindset as me and were very accepting of my connection to my son. It had now been three years since Blake had died. As we followed a trail, we came upon a hollowed-out tree. I had to stop as it reminded me of a tree in my backyard that the kids used to love to go inside, especially Blake. I had a picture of him inside that tree when he was about three years old. This one was big enough for an adult, so I slipped inside. I had the most incredible surge of energy and felt Blake all around me. Tears streamed down my face as I shouted, "He's here! He's here!" I felt a sensation of sheer bliss, joy, and elation. His energy was all around me. I could feel him surround me with love. With that, a monarch butterfly flew by, and my friend, a spiritual healer, said the monarch would be the totem through which Blake would forever appear to me. And she was right.

Until that moment, I had not realized that he had already come to me as a monarch—actually as hundreds of monarchs. The summer after he died, I took a walk down to our local beach. Something I had done countless times. I had never really noticed that monarchs were "a thing" where I lived. I mean, I had certainly seen them, but not in great numbers at all—usually one or two at a time and even then, not very often. But this walk to the beach caught me by surprise. As I got closer, I noticed a few monarchs, then more, then, looking in the distance, there were hundreds of them flying all around. I did not connect Blake to this onslaught of butterflies, but I do remember that it was sometime between his birthday and his death day. I did not realize the connection until a few years later in Red Rock.

Another time after Las Vegas, I was in California, hiking near Ojai. I was by myself, just enjoying the fresh air, when I came upon a butterfly. It was sitting on a branch with its wings folded. At this point, I had not seen monarchs with their wings folded very often, as I mainly saw them flying. I went up close to this one and spoke to it, "Come on, Blake, open your wings!" It stayed right where it was and opened its wings. I just stood there dumbstruck, and a tremendous wave of gratitude washed over me. Neither the butterfly nor I moved for several minutes.

There are quite a few other butterfly stories, as you can imagine. Suffice it to say that now, whenever I see a monarch, I know it is Blake just saying hello.

My goal in attending all those conferences was to learn how to run and expand a business in "this day and age" (mind you, it was 1990 when I had my previous business). I certainly accomplished that, but something else happened as well. It became very clear to me that I needed to write a book.

Needing to do something and actually sitting down and doing it are two totally different things. Finally, I signed up for the Hay House Writer's Workshop, which I knew would be a catalyst. Hay House offered to pub-lish one outline submission from the group that had signed up, and I was determined to be that chosen one. Working very closely with my business coach, E, who was also my writing editor and best friend, I submitted a full outline and chapter summaries for my book about fitness after forty-five. I did not get the publishing offer, but I now had a working outline—halfway there, right?

Not even close! I don't know exactly when it happened, but when it was clear I was not picking up the ball to get the book written, Blake came to me again over my right shoulder, this time a little annoyed yet pleading, "Just write the f***ing book, Mom. Just write the f***ing book!" Even with that push of love and light, I procrastinated—got wrapped up in work, day-to-day responsibilities, and taking care of my mom, who was now ninety-four.

Slowly, I made progress. I would write and send it to E for editing; she would send it back; I would re-write and send it to another friend, who would edit and send it back to me for the final rendering. This went on for all twelve chapters. We were getting there. Then, out of the blue, with no apparent cause, my dear business coach, editor, and, most importantly, best friend, died at the age of sixty-one. She just stopped breathing one day. And she was gone. (Her story is in *Shining A Light on Grief, Book One*)

That completely threw me and stopped me for a good year—all through Covid. Blake respected that time I needed, but he wasn't far away. He was determined to get his mama to finish this book. The story of what happened next is taken from my book's "This Is No Ordinary Dedication":

The real push, the final push, came in February 2022. I responded to a new member of the BodSpir® Membership Program with a simple welcome email. This was her reply:

Hi Elizabeth!

I found you through a very persistent butterfly. A few months ago, I was out for a walk with one of the children I nanny. Ever since I turned 50, I have been having issues with stamina and knew I needed to find a proper exercise program. During that walk, a monarch butterfly was very present and persistent in making sure that I not only acknowledged its presence but spoke to it out loud. So, the 3-year-old I was with and I started to talk to the butterfly. We told it how beautiful it was and how grateful we were to see it. It followed us all the way home. Once in the driveway, the butterfly flew to the back of my car and landed on the dealership sticker on my trunk—Blake Motors. It was then that I realized and said, "Blake!! Is that you?" It was then that it flew right to me and landed on my right shoulder. Boy oh boy, was that a happy cry.

That night I was in front of my computer. I logged onto YouTube and what do I see but a thumbnail for a "Fitness After 45" chat with Elizabeth Phinney. So here I am. Sent by Blake.

I have collected my accessories that were suggested by you and now I begin this journey.

I hope you and all you love are well!

Best wishes,
Sandi (First Nanny to Blake)

Her response completely astounded me. I was dumbstruck! I began shaking with anticipation at the idea that Blake had connected with her and got her to connect with me. I could not believe the dedication that he obviously had in my getting this book completed. I had not really even thought of Sandi since she stopped being Blake's nanny when he was still a small baby. I wrote her back immediately:

Needless to say, I am in a bit of shock after reading your email. Not just from all the synchronicities leading you to me but also in the fact that Blake comes to me as a monarch butterfly!! He is remarkable and tenacious, for sure!

We set up a Zoom call for the next Thursday night. In firming that up, I said:

I will send you the link right before 7:00 pm on Thursday! Will be fascinating, as our conversation evolves, to learn why Blake wanted to get us together! See you soon!

But it was her reply that took everything way beyond synchronicity to actual proof that she was truly in communication with him:

I agree! However, I do think it has something to do with a book that needs
to be written.

"A BOOK THAT NEEDS TO BE WRITTEN?" Was she kidding?
Had he really gone that far to find her to make sure that I would "just write
the f***ing book!"?

Needless to say, once I learned the extent to which Blake had gone
to get me to finish the book, I got right to it and found the discipline I
needed to complete the project, my labor of love!!

I later learned that the day Sandi first came across the butterfly was
August 28, Blake's birthday.

It is to my dear son, Blake, that this book is dedicated. His death gave
me a strength of character that I never knew existed inside of me. And his
persistent support and determination to get his mother to write this book
show a love so powerful that it literally crossed dimensions."

Sandi has become a good friend now, and she sends me texts with
Blake's messages or instructions. Or, whenever we Zoom or phone chat, he
often pops in on the conversation. Or, he has come to her in a dream, and
she will contact me so we can contextualize the information she received.
She has the gift of conversations with Blake. I have the gift of short but
sweet messages. I am so grateful for her return to my life and the endless
gifts she has given me in my communications and connection with Blake.
Although I know that Blake is always around me and I can speak with him
anytime, knowing that I can connect with him through her for clarifica-
tion is the biggest gift that anyone could have given to me. *Her* presence
has enlivened *his* presence in my life, and I am filled with gratitude every
day.

The light on my grief is the constant presence of my son. I know
this is a profound blessing, as most people who lose loved ones do not
realize they can have the same experience. What I have learned is that
those on the other side are always there and are watching and participating
when they are supposed to. I know that Blake is responsible for most of the
synchronicities in my life and is having a blast setting these things up. His
silliness and sense of humor are intact, as well as his cunning and love of a
good scheme. I laugh almost daily at the world and how it presents itself

to me, knowing that he is making sure everything that is meant to happen to me and for me will, indeed, happen.

As for my book—the manuscript has been sent to the publisher with hopes for its release before the summer. Although it has been over six years in the making, I know that everything happens as it is supposed to. And when the book is released, I know that Blake will have as much of a part in spreading its message as I will.

In sharing my story, I hope to give *you* hope—that you, too, can live your life in the company of your lost loved one. I know that Blake is here with me, but I had to *believe* he could be here because it is the belief that allows our connection to happen. So be more aware of how things happen for you. Trust in how things unfold for you day after day. Ask for signs, and then be aware and open-minded. Know that those you love who have passed over are watching and loving you. They are right there with you, just in a different dimension. So, just let go of your doubts and open your heart. Trust … and believe.

CHAPTER 9

Life Turns on a Dime

In honor of Abigail.

By Kelly White

I had heard it said that life turns on a dime, and I can remember thinking on occasion, "What does that even mean?" The day I learned the true meaning of that phrase was a Friday in November of 2012. My youngest daughter, Abigail, was a senior in high school; her older sister, Emily, was a junior in college dreaming of becoming a lawyer; my husband, Dave, was in his mid-40s working sixty hours a week driving tractor trailers, and I was in my early-40s attempting to work my way up the corporate ladder. The day my life turned on a dime was the day I learned Abigail had planned to take her own life.

I remember the day with uncanny clarity. It was a typical Friday morning. Dave had left for work hours before my alarm was set to go off. I had an opportunity to attend a training at work, and Abigail called in one of her three excused days. At the beginning of each school year, starting from when the girls were old enough to stay home alone, they were given three excused days. Think of them as three get-out-of-jail-free passes with no questions asked and no illness required. Other than those three days, the only way they were getting out of school was if they were bleeding, vomiting, or had a fever over a hundred degrees. So they were very careful with those days, and her using one didn't trigger any red flags.

So off I went, footloose and fancy-free, excited about my day. After all, it was a Friday, and I was attending a training instead of my normal day of troubleshooting over the phone. About two hours into the training, my boss knocked on the door of the conference room, requesting I step out to speak with him for a moment. I groaned to myself, thinking, "Great ... someone called in sick, and I have to go help out on the phone."

When I got out into the hall, he told me that Abigail's school counselor had been trying to get a hold of me all morning, and she finally called the operator requesting to speak with my boss. I remember asking him, "Why would the school be calling me?" Abigail was at home enjoying her get-out-of-jail-free pass, and I had called the school on my way to work to let them know she wouldn't be in. "I have no idea, but it sounds important," he said. With my mind fixated on the words, "It sounds important," I collected my things and found a quiet corner to call the school.

The school counselor came on the line and asked me to come to the school. "Abigail had been making threats." I had a whole dialogue in my mind before I even responded ("What do you mean she has been making threats? She is a second-degree black belt and knows full well that you only use those skills in self-defense. She is a straight-A student, treasurer of the class, has never been in trouble before, and is literally nice to everyone. Plus, she isn't even in school today!"). That last thought pulled me out of my head and back to the conversation. "How is this possible? She is home from school today, and what kind of threats?" Nothing could have prepared me for her answer. "Threats of harm to herself, and she is at school now because it was brought to our attention that she has a plan to take her own life."

The drive to her school is the only part of this day that is a blur. One minute I was in my boss's office telling him there was an emergency at her school, and forty minutes later, I had my hand on the front door of the school. I made my way to the main office, and I was escorted to the principal's office by the receptionist, who happened to be a girl I played softball with when I was in high school. The fact that she wasn't a stranger should have been comforting, but the sympathy in her eyes felt more like a reality slap than a warm hug.

When I entered the office, Abigail was sitting at a small round table with the principal and school counselor. She looked at me as the door opened. Then she quickly bowed her head, diverting her eyes to the ground like she was ashamed to look at me. She looked so afraid I just wanted to grab her into my arms and squeeze her tight. Abigail was my snuggler. At that moment, though, she looked like she couldn't bear to be touched.

I stood there looking at her as she stared at the floor. I was flooded with feelings: relief, gratitude, love, pride, horror, guilt, shame, helplessness, fear, anger, determination … I was paralyzed in place with them for what felt like a long time. In reality, it was probably only a few seconds before Mrs. Bennet, the principal, took hold of my elbow and guided me into a chair.

There we sat for over an hour. The counselor explained that her best friend had come to the office that morning afraid for Abigail, how they had coached her friend by coaxing her to school via text, and then they laid out the plan she had to end the pain I didn't even realize she was in.

Abigail had had two major hip surgeries over the previous two years, so there was plenty of prescription pain medication in the house. She was going to take those pills that night while my husband and I were having dinner at my parent's home. I looked at the clock, and it was only noon, and I thought, "How can it only be noon? Why didn't we throw away those pills? Why is she so afraid? Why does she want to leave me? How am I going to tell Dave? What now?". As I write this, my chest is tight with the memory of the pain and horror I felt at that moment, and a single tear is sliding down my cheek just like the stream of them that fell that day.

It wasn't long before the question of what now was answered. The principal informed us that we needed to go to an emergency services facility and that she wouldn't be allowed back at the school until it was deemed safe for her to return. "How could this be happening?"

On to emergency services we went, which is where we met with our very first psychiatrist. During this meeting, I learned that Abigail had formulated this plan weeks ago and had almost come close to carrying it out on several occasions. While we were waiting to learn what facility we were going to for treatment, the psychiatrist asked, "What kept you from following through?" I watched as Abigail tried to work it out in her mind. Then she looked at me for what felt like the first time that day and responded, "Each time I came close to executing my plan and actually writing the note I had written a million times in my head, I had the thought that no one would truly miss me, except Mom. Mom would be devastated. It would break her."

How could someone be so wrong and so right all in the same sentence? I was most definitely not the only person who would miss her but devastated was exactly what I would have been. Honestly, at that moment, I was devastated. I felt alone. Like the literal weight of the world was on my shoulders, and I had no idea how I was going to carry it. I just knew I would … no matter what.

The next stop was the treatment center Abigail would be attending. At this point, I still didn't know if I was going to be allowed to take her home with me. She couldn't start the day program until Monday, and the thought of having her out of my sight was terrifying. We went through an evaluation process, and I swore up and down that she would not be left alone for a minute, that all the pills in our house would be thrown away or stored in a lock box as soon as we got home, and that every moment of the weekend would be spent at home dotting on her.

Abigail didn't want to be separated from me yet, either. In the end, they agreed to let her come home for the weekend, but first, they showed her where she would be spending her days while enrolled in the day program. I pushed down the panic I felt as they walked away and called my husband.

I hadn't been able to bring myself to do it all day. He was on the road, and I didn't want him behind the wheel of an 18-wheeler when I told him this news. He had no words. He was just as blindsided and torn apart as I was. Looking back now, I can see that he was and still is our rock. His love, support, and belief in Abigail and me are unwavering.

Monday came, and we were buzzed in through a locked door. First up was a meeting with the psychiatrist who would be handling Abigail's med management while she was part of the program. I was given a prescription for her meds and told it was time to leave her for SIX HOURS.

I walked past the staff member manning the door, heard the lock click behind me, and I made my way to the car with my heart in a vise as it registered that I had just left my baby girl in a locked ward. My days were spent going in and out that damn door and attempting to work between drop off and pick up, which was virtually impossible. My mind was elsewhere. Nights were spent with her snuggled into my side on the couch until it was time to attempt to sleep. My bed was now an air mattress on the floor in her room. It was two and a half weeks before Abigail was able to return to school, three and a half months before she trusted herself enough to sleep in a room alone, and goodness knows how long it was before I stopped wandering to her room in the middle of the night to reassure myself that she was still there.

During these months, the outside world just kept spinning normally as I attempted to navigate this new reality. It was as if everyone around me was just waiting for things to get back to normal. Waiting for Abigail and me to get back to who we were before life turned on a dime. Thinking back on it, I was also waiting for things to get back to normal. Getting back to normal was the goal. As I typed that last sentence, my mind released a knowing chuckle. There was no going back, but that did not stop us from trying.

That year Abigail was diagnosed with OCD, depressive disorder, panic disorder, and generalized anxiety disorder. She saw a therapist weekly and a psychiatrist monthly, while her cocktail of psych meds and sleep aids was ever-changing.

Despite all of this, she held the lead in the school musical, sang in an acapella group, continued on as treasurer of the senior class, toured colleges, took AP exams, ran track, attended senior trips, graduated from high school fifth in her class, received the good citizenship award, numerous scholarships, and was accepted to multiple college honor programs. In the fall, she attended Hofstra University.

Basically, she went back to wearing the mask of normal for a year and a half, and most of the world went back to expecting it from her. Me included. Even though every time I hugged her, I felt her body tremble. As her freshman year of college went on, I started to notice her hands now trembled, not just her body. The black rings under her eyes were returning. She knew I was starting to see behind the mask she was trying to hold in place, so she withdrew from me. She barely called and rarely came home, and when we did see her, she made sure to have a college friend with her to deflect attention. She was set squarely in denial mode, and when anyone asked if things were going okay and if she was still seeing her therapist at school … she lied.

Although Dave and I never really spoke about it out loud to each other, we knew there was a storm brewing. It was just like the Harry Potter "he who shall not be named" mentality. As long as they didn't speak about Voldemort, his return was not a reality. We were trying the same thing. As long as we just kept moving forward, everything was fine. Maybe we could outrun the storm.

The thing about denial, though, is you can only keep it up for so long. Eventually, the storm comes.

This particular storm surfaced when we were on an annual New York City family trip over Christmas break. For a few years now, our family and my sister's family had been going to NYC for a few days between Christmas and New Year's. This was the first year we decided to spend the money to stay right in the heart of the city. I always looked forward to this trip!

This year though, on the morning of the first day, Abigail woke with what we thought was a stomach bug. She barely left the hotel room the entire time we were there. On the afternoon of our last night there, she finally got up the nerve to tell us what was going on. She had been arrested for smoking marijuana in a Target parking lot. A court date had already been set, and a parent had to be present.

Dave and I just stared at each other across the room as she sobbed in my arms. The questions and fear just hung in the air. All the feelings of that day in the principal's office were back present and accounted for.

As I write this, I am still trying to decide what was more alarming to me back then. Was it that her panic disorder and OCD were so out of control that she had been throwing up for days? Maybe it was the look on Emily and my sister's faces when I told them. Or the fact that my mother was not a safe space for me. The thought of her finding out Abigail had been arrested was paralyzing to me. To be honest, it is still something I have never told her. Was it that my child had been placed in handcuffs, fingerprinted, and placed in a jail cell? No, it was the realization that I, too, was not a safe space for my child. Her subconscious mind decided it was better to vomit for three days than it was to just tell me.

Before this trip, Dave and I had already been making moves to get her to come home from school. The log cabin we built, aka our "forever home," had been sold. We moved a little over an hour south just that November and rented a cute coastal home in Jamestown, RI. After the trip to NYC, she agreed it was a good idea for her to take the semester off and regroup.

The first month she was home, Abigail barely spoke or moved. She went from bed to the couch and back again. Meanwhile, I found her a new therapist and a lawyer. By the time her semester off was over, we had been to court, where thankfully, she received a suspended sentence. She was performing at a little dinner theater, and the light was slowly starting to come back into her eyes. She was smiling again.

For me, though, the anxiety and fear were starting to take their toll on me physically and mentally. I ended up on short-term disability for a few weeks with a nervous condition I could no longer hide. My return to work was gradual and difficult. I just could not be away from her for any significant length of time. My nervous system would not tolerate being outside of my bubble. After almost two years of this, my therapist submitted a request for an official accommodation to work from home full time, and my employer eventually agreed. I was beyond relieved, but the process left me hurt and disillusioned.

When Dave and I sold our house, our ultimate plan was to move to North Carolina. I knew I would be able to work remotely if we moved that far away and his company had a hub there he could transfer to. We thought Jamestown would be a temporary stop. We would stay long enough to get Abigail home, and our families were used to us not living so close.

During the eighteen months we lived in Jamestown, Abigail decided to commute to college, and her boyfriend was visiting more frequently. Emily was attending law school in Boston, which was close enough for visits, and my family decided that they were going to move closer to us and the ocean. By the time our lease was up, my sister's family of four, my mom & dad, and my sister/brother-in-law all lived within ten to twenty minutes from us. So, we decided to stay and buy a house in Rhode Island. Life was starting to feel familiar again. Almost normal. There's that word again.

The home we bought was a raised ranch with a large finished room and full bathroom downstairs that had its own entry. So, we built a bedroom in the garage. When I say we, I mean Dave and my Dad built a bedroom in the garage. It was perfect for Abigail to have some independence while also having the security of being just a staircase away. I'm not sure which one of us needed that security more.

After a semester or two, Abigail decided that college was not for her. I remember smiling to myself after she told me. She was learning her limits, letting go of the plan, and finding HER way. She was still with her high school sweetheart, and eventually, he moved into the downstairs space with her, and they started planning a future together. For a while, I allowed myself to believe that the move to Rhode Island was exactly the reset we all needed.

I believed it right up until the day Emily graduated from law school. She walked across that stage, and in my mind, I was in awe of her. Pride doesn't even come close to the thoughts that were spinning in my head. Graduation day was absolutely fabulous, and I enjoyed every moment of it. The problem is I barely felt any of it due to my medication mix. Here I was watching the beautiful girl who made me a mother graduate from law school, and I was basically Spock on Star Trek. All thought and very little emotion.

I wasn't living … I was surviving, and I wanted to live again.

The truth is, I was still living in my bubble. I barely left the house for fear my digestive system would betray me. My chest tightened, and my mind frantically looked for a way out at the first sign of any kind of intense emotion, despite the fact that I was emotionally numbed by medication. It had been five years since that Friday in November, and I still didn't feel safe. I was still trying to outrun the darkness, terrified that it would catch us. Still denying the fact that it had already caught us … five years ago.

Looking back, I now realize a lot of what I was going through was grief. I was grieving the loss of the life I thought we were going to have. The family relationships that were breaking under the pressure. The career that I had dedicated years to I no longer wanted. There was loss all around me, and I was slowly moving through the stages of grief. After five years, I was saying goodbye to the stages known as denial and saying hello to anger.

I was angry with my mother. I had been living with the weight and fear that if I missed a sign, I could lose my child. My mother didn't believe the danger was even real. Her belief was that God knew losing a grandchild wasn't something she could handle; therefore, it wasn't going to happen. The problem was, "I just couldn't move on."

I was angry at most of my family. For pointing out all the ways Abigail was letting them down instead of noticing all her little victories. For thinking it was their job to point out that, at times, Abigail was manipulating me. Like they somehow had a clue what it was like to walk in my shoes or know what it felt like to be your child's emotional lifeline.

They had stopped believing in us, and I was wasting energy trying to get them to. I wanted them to see what I saw. An amazing, compassionate scared sick girl who just needed extra space, grace, and time to find her way.

I was also angry with Abigail. For every time she stopped therapy or medications shortly after we would make it through a rough patch. I was angry at myself most of all for a whole host of things. The anger didn't last long. There was no time or energy for anger.

The next five years were very different. I was still in the thick of it, but there had been a mindset shift. I was no longer trying to outrun what I had come to refer to as the darkness. Instead, I decided we would invite it to dinner, ask a few questions, and get to know it better. What were these things we were trying to medicate into submission? Why were we so scared and ashamed of them? Why were we fighting so hard to hide them and be "normal"?

One of the first things we learned at this dinner was that we had no idea how to talk to each other about what we were feeling. Especially the darker, more emotionally charged feelings. In our world, emotions were something to be hidden. Something we felt but did not share. Sharing meant you were being dramatic, too sensitive, or you had no coping skills.

Abigail experiences intrusive thoughts with major highs and lows. I also experience intrusive thoughts. We both feel emotions very strongly. Emotions that, historically, had been labeled as shameful. So, we made a pact. We would never hide our dark parts from each other again. We would learn how to look at them and talk to each other about them. Another shift had happened. I was no longer trying to fix things for Abigail. We were now a team. A mother-daughter team.

Since we had determined emotions weren't shameful, it was probably okay to feel them again. So, we both weaned off of our psych medications with the doctor's help. Through individual and joint cognitive behavioral therapy, we figured out that medication was still needed. One that would subdue intrusive thoughts without stifling emotions. First, we needed to find a psychiatrist that was willing to really work with us, not just throw meds at us. I am not going to lie; this process isn't a cakewalk. Navigating the mental health arena is an absolute shit show. In the end, finding the right psychiatrist fit was a game changer. We had found another piece of the puzzle.

Coexisting with mental illness has been a bit of a dance. Sometimes you take the lead, and other times it does. The trick is learning what triggers the illness to steal back the lead. When we do lose the lead, we have learned to be gentle with ourselves. It only seems to keep the lead longer when we try to deny, hide, battle, or bargain our way out of it. Instead, we have learned to embrace what I have come to learn is the final stage of grief, acceptance. We do our best to accept, honor, and love all of ourselves through it. This includes accepting and honoring our grief and mental illness.

My hope for you as you read this chapter is that you feel less alone. That you begin to see that everyone grieves in their own way and their own time, which is completely okay. That there is no right or wrong way to grieve. I don't have the ability to write my ten-years-ago self a letter, but if I could, it would sound something like this. Maybe one of the tools that helped us along our healing journey will also help you.

> Dear Kelly,
>
> I know this is hard, and I am sorry that you are going through this. Be gentle with yourself. You are grieving, and learning how to live with grief and mental illness takes time. I am happy to say that after ten years, I feel like we are out of danger. When we lay our heads on the pillow at night now, there is no part of us that fears losing Abigail to her mental illness.
>
> Here are some of the things that have helped us heal.
> - Finding the right therapist, psychiatrist, and medication was key. Don't give up. You will find the right fit.
> - Day programs and group therapy.
> - Realizing that the feelings that come with grief and mental illness are not shameful or bad. They do not need to be fixed or hidden. They need to be honored and accepted.

- Stop trying to get back to normal. There is no such thing.
- You cannot heal while you are trying to live for everyone else.
- Nobody knows your daughter better than you and Dave. Trust yourselves and stop caring what other people think. Yes, this includes family.
- Accepting that there is no right way to grieve/heal and no time limit. Everyone's journey is unique.
- Abigail's mental illness and happiness are not your responsibility. It is hers. You can walk with her, though.
- Read other people's stories. It will help you feel less alone.
- Accepting that you do not get over grief or mental illness. You learn to walk with them.
- Learning how to have healthy and compassionate conversations with each other is crucial.

This journey has taught us that we can do hard things. That we can only control ourselves. To love all of yourself unconditionally. Flaws and all. To try and live life expecting nothing and appreciating everything. For that, I am forever grateful.

Love,
Me

CHAPTER 10

The Unspoken

In memory of Carly Rose.

By Chelsea Force

Part One: No One Wants To Be a Part of This Club

I thought I understood pain and loss until these events struck me so deep within my core that they changed me altogether. These experiences also taught me the full depth of human emotion and love through loss, support, and an incredible resilience that I didn't know the human heart was capable of.

Chances are, you are reading this because you are part of a grieving club that no one wants to belong to, but somehow it is still helpful to know you are NOT alone. So, thank you for being here. Thank you for your openness to listen or read about others' journeys, your willingness to empathize, and your strength in connecting even when it's difficult.

Hopefully, by the end of this chapter, you will feel the strength of a heart, and you will know that even in the darkest moments, when the hole from a loss feels so deep, the heart can still beat, and you can still find purpose. This story will highlight just one version of the intense roller coaster so many moms go through on their journey to build their families. Hopefully, together, we can shed light on the gap between keeping things to yourself (not to *burden* others) and allowing yourself the time and grace it takes to support your mental and emotional well-being.

While writing this chapter, I am in the midst of "it" all. My story is about child loss, both during pregnancy (miscarriage) and at birth (stillborn). This is about the hurt, the hopelessness, and the need for help. It's also about the strength, support, and small things that make a big difference. As I sit here writing this with burning eyes and intense pains coursing through my body, I am going through another miscarriage. Just a few days ago, I was talking with my family about how grateful and excited we were to grow our family. I was 6.5 weeks along and beaming with pride and love, and I could hardly wait to announce it to our friends, family members, and the world. It is something we have wanted for a long time. My hesitation to share the good news came from the feeling of fear, not knowing, and being worried that the loss could happen again … and it did.

If you have had the misfortune of a loss in miscarriage, first let me say I am so sorry. I send a warm hug and healing thoughts. Most of the time, this experience is terribly painful and lonely (both physically and emotionally). There is a major societal problem in dealing with this specific type of loss. So many people suffer alone, and miscarriage is so very common. We are taught and told to "wait to tell anyone" when we are pregnant.

Why is that? Does it help the baby for no one to know? Does it help the mother or the father (especially as new parents) to try and navigate quietly like secret agents through a thirteen-week trimester of new fears and feelings, along with sickness and exhaustion? Does it help to prepare or understand what is about to happen? NO. It doesn't help anyone to be lonely. It doesn't help anyone to sneak around being dishonest and hiding what we are going through, especially if others around us would be so willing to help.

What *DOES* this "keep it quiet" mandate do? It alienates a new, nervous pregnant mom. It forces her to hide her body, as if ashamed, while she begins to go through a magical, miraculous transition. The beginning of pregnancy is full of ALL of the emotions. It is terrifying, wonderful, exhausting, and a miracle all at once. It should be celebrated, and yet most people painstakingly hide it through the entire first three months. They keep it quiet and wonder on their own how to navigate new feelings and a new body, and when the worst happens (as it does in an estimated twenty-six percent of pregnancies for women in their thirties), they are ISOLATED and hide their pain from those around them.

Since everyone is told to "wait to tell people," society is never *inconvenienced* by hearing about the pain and the loss. Both parents are left to hide their pain, and since no one knows, they put on a smile through the hardest moments. As a mom, I have even experienced feelings of guilt when dealing with a miscarriage. I felt guilty about missing work and backing out of plans without a full honest explanation. I felt guilty that my body failed me, and I felt guilty that I wasn't allowing myself proper time to grieve. This needs to be talked about … so at the very least, I'm here to say you are NOT alone. Many others have felt this pain. I know this pain, and I know the challenge of hiding while I heal. While I know this societal structure needs to be torn down, here I sit with quiet tears in my eyes. I suppose writing this is a start and a hope to help someone else feel heard and seen. I see you.

Part Two: The Reveal

My story starts out with one of the highest, most exciting moments of my life. After a long time of waiting, planning, and preparing, my husband and I finally decided to start our family. A short time later, we found out that our dreams had come true, and not only were we pregnant, we were having TWINS! It was like we were living in a fairy tale story, and we couldn't have been happier.

We waited so anxiously for the doctors to tell us it was the right time to share the news. When both babies continued to receive great reports at frequent weekly ultrasounds, we were given the green light to let everyone know. Being our first pregnancy, we had elaborate plans to tell everyone, and our gender reveal (revealing both the gender AND the fact that it was TWINS) went viral on YouTube.

Only our parents and siblings knew that it was twins, which made the reveal two times the surprise! Our friends and family packed in to join in on the excitement. In your regular gender-reveal style, the room was decorated with pink and blue everything where people could vote, right down to the candy bars where they could choose "nuts" or "no nuts" for fun.

The votes were in, and we were ready to open the box and unleash the balloons! Just before we did, Matt removed his polo to unveil his t-shirt that he was ever-so proud of, revealing it was twins! Everyone gasped, clapped, cried, and laughed. We shared that we knew they were going to be identical twins, so either both boys or girls. When we ripped open the box, and the pink balloons erupted, my heart just about burst with excitement. That moment set off a constant trail of dreaming of a life with our two little girls.

Our friends and family shared in our excitement! My brain raced day in and day out about how much I already loved these identical twin girls! We planned everything from the schedules to home rearrangement and set up, and researched everything there was to possibly research about twins. I joined every mom's group and every community to learn and share with other twin moms. I could not have been more proud and excited to be moving to this next exciting stage of life.

The pregnancy was not easy, and it seemed to last forever. Despite all of the symptoms, dizziness, nausea, and headaches, I felt so strong, and I was amazed at what my body was doing. My husband, Matt, and I spoke to the girls daily, and they kicked with excitement and kept me up all night, every night. The kicking also provided such a sense of connection. They were constantly shifting and flipping. The doctors were always amazed at the movement, and everything continued to progress on track. I could not wait to hold them in my arms.

The nursery at home was set up with white double mini cribs. There were identical pink and white blankets hung by each one, hand-knit by their great-grandmother. The door, trim, and one wall were painted pink with sparkles shining through the paint. There were decals with quotes about strong girls on the walls. The curtains and pillows were pink and black with superhero logos and flowers throughout. The clothes and matching wonder woman outfits were hung in the closet with care. Their names were hung above each crib in hand-painted letters on the wall (Carly & Chloe). The matching purple car seats with Minnie Mouse seat mirrors were installed. We were ready.

Part Three: The Unthinkable

At 36 weeks and four days, the unthinkable happened.

I started to feel sick. Something wasn't right. The girls' movement was still there but had slightly slowed. I tried to lie down, but something told me to get to the hospital right away. Just two days earlier, we had received a perfect eleven-point bill of health for both girls, and everything was looking great. We were told everyone was growing healthy and on track …

We rushed to the emergency room, and they took my vitals right away. As we sat and waited, my heart was racing. I had been in that room a few times before with some other strange symptoms, but nothing prepared me for what came next.

They came in for the ultrasound, as they normally did. Following the regular routine, everything was hooked up and plugged in, and two separate monitors were put on. As mentioned, the girls were early gymnasts and loved to flip around, so it always took a while to get a reading on both heartbeats. Except … The second reading never showed up.

Three different doctors tried, and in complete ignorance, I sat and waited for the next person to try. The doctors were dropping hints that things may not be okay, and I never picked up on it. I was 100% just waiting for them to tell me everything was fine and that we could go on our way. Finally, the head doctor came in, sat down next to my legs, grabbed my hand, and told me that "baby A" (Carly) no longer had a heartbeat.

The room went dark, and my head was spinning. For sure, she was wrong! She had to be wrong! I stepped off the hospital bed and fell to the floor. My husband came over to help, but we were both doubled over with heartache. I couldn't breathe, I couldn't see, my blood pressure dropped, and I was in shock. I was screaming for help. Someone do something! Someone help save my babies! My body began to shake, and I could hear mumbling voices and doctors saying they were going to send me for an emergency C-section.

I couldn't catch my breath to speak, but all I could think of was, "Please save my babies!" The next seconds felt like hours. After the longest wait, my heart shattering further with every second, and the sounds of only one heart beating on the monitor echoing through the room, I realized someone was trying to get my attention. They asked us if there was someone we should call to tell or come to help. Absolutely not. Telling someone would mean it was real, and it just couldn't be really happening. I was sent in for surgery.

My mind raced … How could this happen? What have I done wrong? How could my body betray me? Are they going to be able to save Carly? Is Chloe going to be okay? I would've given absolutely anything, including my life, to save theirs. Doctors rushed around in what felt like a muffled blurry chaos. My husband, who I know, felt the loss and heartbreak as much as me, gripped me tightly, and somehow stayed strong while I was unraveling. I couldn't stand or move. He held me upright enough for the doctors to deliver the epidural for surgery.

This was supposed to be the best moment of our lives … Once the C-section was complete, the doctors whisked the babies away. I was unreasonable. I fought and yelled for someone to try to save Carly. Why weren't they even trying? I asked for CPR or a defibrillator. I needed to fight with everything I had just in case there was a chance. They quietly assured me that it was too late. Everything was blurry and dark. I could not control the shaking, sobbing, or breathing in my own body. Chloe was rushed away before I even got to hug her. Carly and I were transported to a separate room. It was dark and lonely. The doctor said some things (my brain couldn't comprehend anything), placed Carly on my chest, void of heartbeat or life, and left the room quickly.

I had never felt so crushed, lost, confused and alone. I'm quite sure someone may have told me, but I had no recollection or idea of where Chloe or my husband were rushed to, and I couldn't believe that they left *us* alone. I had never touched a lifeless body before and just could not wrap my brain around that this was my daughter and this was reality. I gazed down at her perfect little round face. Rosy cheeks, red lips, and the most angelic face in a tiny pink hat. Her silence was deafening. I tried to keep my tears from soaking her as I held her for what would likely be the first and only time.

I yelled for the nurse and pleaded for someone to come back. I was bleeding, cold, shaking uncontrollably, terrified, and broken. Thoughts raced and yet crashed all at the same time. For the first time ever in my life, even suicidal thoughts invaded my brain, along with terrifying thoughts of losing Chloe too. My instincts as a new mother roared in a dangerous way. I was willing to take any measure to try and be there for my girls. If I threw myself off of the table, could I somehow join Carly and be with her?

Time passed at a snail's pace, and what may have been minutes felt like an eternity. Eventually, the nurse came back in and reassured me that my husband was with Chloe in the NICU and I would be there with them soon. Still unable to breathe, I tried to speak. Was she okay? I couldn't muster the words. What if the answer was no?

The doctors asked again about notifying others. My heart was broken and shattered all over again. How could we even say it? How would life possibly go on from here? Matt was strong enough to have already taken on the burden of telling our parents what had happened. They raced over immediately to be there for support in some way.

Part Four: The NICU

Finally, we received assurance that Chloe was stable at the moment, but it became clear we would all be there for a while. She was six weeks early. While they monitored her lung development, ability to eat, and body temperature, we never left her side. She was connected to what seemed like a hundred monitor chords and an IV. She was inside a glass incubator and out of reach. The screens behind the incubator flashed and beeped with every slight change in breathing, temperature, or heartbeat change. Every few minutes, small alarms went off, and our hearts dropped with each sound.

The constant heart rate monitor was a steady, painful reminder of the perfect tiny daughter we lost and her sudden missing heartbeat. Sleep only came from occasionally drifting off in a weak state of tears and exhaustion. We continued to wait, silently listening to every monitor flash, beep, and siren twenty-four hours a day. The nurses and doctors rushed in and out. The only way he could make contact with Chloe was for short periods of time with the help of a nurse or through the holes in the side of the case. It was the longest month of our lives in the NICU.

The things I thought were important before seemed so meaningless all of a sudden. I have regrets. I was too hurt and broken to take pictures. I have so few from the first month of Chloe's life. She was in the incubator. I was so terrified of the monitors and the chords, about something going wrong at any moment. I thought that pictures would forever be reminders of this very real pain. There was no explanation for what happened to Carly. What if it suddenly happened to Chloe too?

I couldn't take a picture when she was out of the incubator, either. She remained attached to all the monitors, feeding, and breathing tubes, and I would have had to be in it. How do I take a picture with my baby girl while I was such an obvious wreck and red and raw from constant tears? Would she look back someday and feel like we weren't happy to hold her? I couldn't even bear to try to smile.

Feeling every emotion in the world made it almost impossible to feel anything at all. It's like every emotion was amplified times a thousand, but each emotion canceled another out. The gratitude and happiness that could've been there to greet Chloe in her first precious moments of life were canceled out by the grief and sorrow of saying goodbye to her sister. The grief and loss could not fully be felt or dealt with since we had to be strong and hopeful and do our best to take care of Chloe, who needed our support. The inner turmoil was numbing.

Anyone who knows me would tell you that I am high-energy, fast-talking, and full of life. Yet, for the first time in my life, I was at a complete loss. I had no words. I had no solutions, no energy, and no idea what the future held. As time went on in the NICU, I grew increasingly afraid of the prospect of tearing down the life we created to try and rebuild a new one. How could we walk in the door and into that pink superhero nursery with two of everything? How could we take down her name and take apart, piece by piece, the second crib? What were we going to do with the matching clothes, all of the "sister" decor, the extra car seat set up with the cute Minnie Mouse mirrors, and all of our thoughts and dreams that had been so vividly planned out over the last eight months?

How could I face my friends and family members and explain what happened when I still couldn't even speak or come to terms with it myself? How could I handle every single interaction where everyone would ask about the twins? I went dark. I stayed off my phone, I never checked messages, and I never went on social media. I wanted to hide. As terrible as it sounds, I didn't want to leave the NICU. I couldn't bear the thought of starting our new family life without Carly.

Meanwhile, our friends and family poured in incredible support. To this day, I feel terrible that my brain cut out bits and pieces of our time there, and it's hard to remember who did what, but I hope they forever know how grateful we were just for the thoughts. I couldn't look at a phone, answer a text or speak to anyone. I was broken.

Would I ever be able to stand up straight again? How could I possibly be strong enough to be the mother my daughter deserved? All I knew was that I needed to take the next tiny step each day. The only thing that mattered was keeping Chloe safe and healthy.

Slowly she began to pass tests, and monitors were removed a little bit at a time after the first three weeks. The incredible team of doctors visited every morning to review each part of her health in an extensive meeting with the nurses. I took notes, asked questions, listened intently, and even argued occasionally. I needed to try and help her in any way I could. Many days it felt like one step forward and two steps back. Eventually, with the feeding and breathing tubes removed, there was finally a small glimmer of hope. When she was moved to a crib, we were able to reach her and finally hold her more often.

I felt like so much time had been robbed already. We could never get back those first three weeks of not cuddling our baby. I knew that I would never want to let her go. I began to try to pick myself up very slowly. I thought about her. We had already missed so much time holding her, and I didn't want the face she was always looking up at to be crying down on her in grief. She deserved better.

While in the NICU, the doctors and nurses were nothing short of amazing. I don't know how they do what they do. They are truly heroes. There was also support offered to the parents in the unit. There were therapy groups. The doctors recommended many times that we sit in on the sessions. I knew we needed to try something. We went to the group meeting and listened to parents whose child was in worse health conditions, parents who were hopeful and had seen great progress, and a few parents with twins who were premature but growing and doing well.

What I'm going to say next is in NO way a discredit to any support groups. I know this could be an amazing way to cope, communicate and connect during a tough time. I will also say that grief is different for everyone, and this did NOT work for me. Any progress I had made (which wasn't much) in the last three weeks was instantly buried back into a well of sorrow. I internalized it all. I was always empathetic to others, but I had changed. I no longer just understood, I had become a deeply-feeling empath, and I could not help but absorb their pain. I felt it ALL. To make it worse, I also felt jealousy. I was so jealous of the parents who were going to be allowed to continue their lives with two healthy living twins. Then, I felt even more broken from the pain and guilt for not being able to make progress when everyone else seemed so much stronger. If you are grieving, please know that there is no one-size-fits-all way to go about your healing.

Part Five: Guilt and Going Home

The day finally came when Chloe was doing well enough to start the tests to be cleared to go home. I feel guilty just sharing this: I actually felt relief when she didn't pass the car seat test. Relief? It meant we were going to stay in those isolated walls with help for our premature daughter another day. It meant that the continuing monitors and alarms would be there to alert us if there was a problem. It meant not facing the reality that we would have to redesign our life plans without our other daughter. We stayed another day. When she passed the next set of tests and was disconnected from the alarms and sensors, I could barely walk to carry her out the door. The floor felt like mud, and my feet were heavy. This was supposed to be a happy moment. Why did I feel so sad, scared, and alone? The car seemed strange. We hadn't been in it in a month. My mom had removed the extra car seat and mirror before we were ready to leave. I sat in the back seat, next to the car seat, in the center, with my hand on Chloe's tiny chest to feel her breathing, and I could not bear to look over at the other empty seat beside me.

Still, we could not possibly go home. We spent the next couple of weeks at my parents' house. It was familiar but far enough away from the nursery and home set up for the twins. People started to visit slowly. I knew they all had only our best interests at heart. They were showing up in support, but I still did not want to see anyone, and I felt like going home would make that happen more, and I still could not face people. They would inevitably ask questions like "How are you doing?" and I wasn't okay. Would there be a need to try to explain? I couldn't.

Chloe was over a month old, hadn't met anyone, and I still wasn't ready to talk. Other people didn't know what to say either. How could they? Even with all the best intentions, they couldn't possibly understand. Some of them said things like, "At least you have Chloe." While I know they probably meant well, it felt like a thousand daggers through the heart. I WAS grateful and so very in love with my daughter, Chloe. I ALSO was so very in love with Carly, who would never be held, heard, or hugged again. My heart didn't understand how to hold on, and my eyes never dried.

As time went on, I tried to force the negativity and despair down. All I could think of was seeing the world through Chloe's eyes. The first experiences should be full of smiles, love, and happy faces looking back at her precious face. Instead, it was hard to look into her eyes, and she saw so much sadness in ours. I had to be better. I had to find a way to be what she needed and deserved.

I began to hold it in and did my best to only cry only in private. It was uncontrollable in the shower or in the car when I was alone. Sometimes I had to pull over to pull myself together. "Pick yourself up, Chelsea. She needs you to be stronger." So, I did.

I truly cannot say enough about the support from our family. They brought food and made sure we ate, helped us redecorate our home to start new, and even shared their own homes. We had some incredible support from friends too. Yes, you certainly learn who your true friends are. This lesson is not always easy. True friends didn't just post pictures to say things online; they showed up. One of our best friends visited four different restaurants, picked up one (or two) of each of our favorite things, and showed up. They just sat and visited. They didn't ask questions, they just were there, and those little things meant a lot.

The next step was to find myself again. Hiding all the crying was *not* a healthy way of dealing with the pain, but it helped me not feel guilty while holding and caring for Chloe. I needed an outlet. I tried more group therapy which wrecked me. It was like the pain multiplied by everyone else's experiences. I felt ALL of their pain and loss. I began to feel it ALL. Every TV show, every book, and every commercial affected my heart and soul in a way I didn't know was possible. I was different. I had to adjust all of the input around us. I changed the TV shows and the music and dove into stories about hope and personal development books.

There is a big part of this that I haven't really mentioned. I wasn't just concerned about my family and my daughter's future but also my own. At the time, I had a career that I absolutely loved. I was helping people and making a difference, and I had always planned on continuing my career as a working mom, and I knew it would make my kids proud too. I was a full-time martial arts instructor at Mastery Martial Arts. This was not your average martial arts program, as I was a motivational teacher for all levels to learn leadership and life skills. I spoke daily with conviction about the "Yes I Can" attitude and the ability to overcome any challenge … This all made sense until now. The problem was me. I was different. How could I ever be that person for others if I was so lost myself?

Have you ever felt like this? Have you ever doubted your ability to find yourself again after loss? If you have, don't give up. Again, everyone's journey through loss is different. What hurt me may be perfect for you, and what works for me may not do the same. Just keep trying. I found an unconventional approach to beginning to heal.

The truth is that my "healing" began when I realized that I would never heal. It was never going to be okay, and it was always going to hurt … but I was going to be "okay."

Luckily, one of the things I had always learned and practiced as an instructor was personal development. I threw myself into personal development and psychology. I learned that human emotions have endless depths like the ocean, and one of the strongest things you can do is sail through that turbulent sea. I read stories of unbelievable trials and tribulations other people had endured and how they managed to overcome and continue to be strong and help others. Although I was not ready to do it yet, I started to see purpose in sharing my story and hope for someday being able to somehow understand and comfort others.

Grieving sometimes does something weird in our society. It can cause people to avoid you like the plague. It's as if the grief would be contagious. I chose to believe that people are generally good and want to be helpful. In a situation like this, there is nothing anyone can do or say to help. I understand and believe that the best thing to do is just be there. Add a hug when you can, and just be present. My husband took some level of support in the messages and response, while I, on the other hand, avoided it completely and wanted people to just not mention anything about what we were going through.

Part Six: The Return

Would I ever be able to go back to the career I loved so much? It felt almost impossible to show my tear-stained face in a place where I had always been full of life and positivity. It was hard to stand there in my broken, swollen body that had betrayed me in a place where I had always felt so strong. I was afraid to be greeted with "I'm sorry." I didn't want more sorrow. I had plenty of my own.

The first steps back into the place I loved so much felt just as difficult as those first steps out of the hospital. Yet, instead of sorrow, I was greeted with warmth, understanding, and support. This wasn't just a group of people; it was a family who were there to help me get back on my feet. I had always tried to lead by positive example and be there to support our families during tough times, but this was a new level of unconditional support. The rest of the staff are people I've grown up with and my instructor since I was seven. It's a unique kind of place, and I knew it was all going to be okay. I was going to be okay. My family was always going to be a part of this family.

Again, I learned something new. Even though I felt so beat down, they didn't look at me as broken or less strong. They saw something I hadn't considered. They saw the strength in being there; they reminded me that progress isn't always pretty and that "Yes I Can" is a way of life. In the middle of the darkness, there was a glimmer of hope, and we were grateful.

Before losing Carly, I was so focused on being strong, capable, and in control of both physicality and emotions. I had built a concrete foundation of strength to walk on, and now I felt like I was stuck in quicksand. Here's the crazy thing: concrete is really an illusion of strength, and it can still be broken and cracked. Once the concrete is cracked, it is almost impossible to put it back together. Quicksand, on the other hand, moves, rebalances, and rejoins itself once a challenge passes through. I began to slowly build a new self-image where being vulnerable and emotional was the real identity of being strong.

This is for you; if you are broken or grieving, you have a new potential for strength inside you. It's the ability to walk in your emotions, not hide from them. The strength comes from feeling all the feels and choosing your response. You can share your strength by showing others how to be the best version of themselves in a beautiful, vulnerable, imperfect way.

This new foundation has been tested for sure.

Part Seven: More Pain

We knew we wanted to continue to grow our family. Within a year after Chloe's birthday and Carly's death, we were blessed with another pregnancy. It was like a beam of light to help our family. Until it wasn't. We suffered a month-two miscarriage. We told no one. Not even our parents or close friends knew what we were going through at the time. We "spared" everyone else the grief and boiled it by ourselves. Again, this is not a recommended way to deal with this type of pain. We needed to rebuild ourselves.

My husband, Matt, and I had not had any time together since Chloe was born. We ran away from it all. We took a chance to use a free trip we had saved up and went away to Las Vegas for the weekend, where I could suffer the physical pain and shed more tears that no one would see. We drowned ourselves in the lights, sights, and sounds the first night, but the only thing I could focus on was the mountains around us. I had been to Vegas before and enjoyed the view, but this time my mind felt connected to the depths of the horizon.

We spent the rest of our trip at the Grand Canyon. The vastness, color, and colossal shapes just seemed to make everything else seem smaller. Much to Matt's dismay, I climbed down a bit to get a better view of the canyon and sat on a rock near the edge. To my surprise, he followed me despite his fear of heights. He sat down next to me on the hot orange rock, looked out ahead, put his arm around my waist, and said, "We are going to be okay." He was right.

While we will always feel the pain and mourn for our children who grew wings before they opened their eyes, we are so grateful for our two beautiful children here on Earth with us, Chloe and Max. Yes, we were so happy to announce, just after Chloe's first birthday, that we were newly expecting and she was going to be a big sister. Every moment was terrifying; every ultrasound and heart rate check was painful. We made it through the longest nine months and had a healthy baby boy who lights up our lives with joy and is his sister's best friend.

As I sit here today in the midst of this familiar, very real pain, dealing with this second miscarriage, I feel my husband's arm around my waist and the heat from the sun bouncing around the vast Grand Canyon. He is still right. We are going to be okay ... and so will you. Don't give up. Tell others about your story, and remember that the best strength comes from the vulnerability to live in your emotions and be true to yourself.

Part Eight: The Funeral

It took us over a year to make plans for Carly's ashes. It sounds terrible to say, but I just couldn't bear to make such permanent decisions. Arrangements made it so real and so final, and it still felt so raw. Her ashes had remained in my husband's parent's home while we tried to wrap our heads around how to "make arrangements." When they say "make arrangements," it always sounds so nonchalant, but if you've ever had to do this for a family member or loved one, you know it is a daunting task with heavy decisions. We were at a standstill. Nothing seemed like the "right" choice because it would just never be RIGHT to let her go.

More loss struck the family the following year when my husband's grandmother passed away. Eventually, we decided that Carly would be buried in a tiny heart-shaped box alongside her great-grandmother so that they could watch out for each other in the next life until we could hold her again. I knew I would not be able to muster up words at the funeral, so I sat up the night before with a tear-drenched face. I took out my computer, paper, and colored pencils, drew her a picture, and wrote to her instead. I left a colored pencil drawing of a detailed Rose (Carly's middle name) with angel wings and this poem with her in the casket:

Have you ever held an angel?
We did from head to toes
So beautiful and perfect
Her name is Carly Rose

Your kicks and flips and playful spirit
Kept us up all night
We didn't know you were growing wings
Getting ready to take flight.

Your time on Earth was far too short
And far from being fair
We will forever feel your love
In our hearts and in the air.

We had planned a whole life with you
And you never got to know
The amazing things you were yet to do
The places you'll never go

You taught us more about the heart
Even when yours ceased to beat.
Grief can tear a heart apart,
Somehow you helped us to our feet.

You kept your sister safe for us
You taught us how to fight
When it didn't seem possible
You guided us through night.

Our angel is here and everywhere
In the breeze, the air, the sun.
She's here along this wild ride
And when the day is done.

Have you ever held an angel?
We did and always do
She is here in spirit all around
Spreading light to me and you.

Have you ever held an angel?
We did and always will
She is here within our hearts and minds
Gave us purpose to fulfill

Have you ever held an angel?
She taught us from the start,
That no matter the difficulties,
You get up and do your part.

Rest In Peace, Carly Rose, my baby girl.

Part Nine: The Most Difficult Conversation

We thought the burial would be the most difficult step of all ... until it sunk in that we would someday need to also share the loss with our kids. How do you decide when the right moment is to steal such innocence and tell them about a lost sibling? How do we tell them without instilling fear while still protecting them from hurt? It took years before we were able to share it with Chloe. I would practice in the car how to have the conversation. I knew that I, at the very least, would need to be able to speak Carly's name in order to have this heavy talk.

There were other reasons we felt like she should know. She had always had trouble sleeping. She needed physical contact to relax from day one. It was easy to blame myself for the sleep troubles (like so many moms do). Once she finally got out of the incubator and out of NICU, we had so much missed time, and I just needed to hold her. Turns out, she needed the physical connection too. After many sleep evaluations and trying all the sleep methods, the sleep therapist finally said to us, "Most likely, she needs the extra physical connection because of her connection with her twin sister in the womb." That was all I needed to hear. We no longer wanted to make her try to sleep separately, and we just allowed the extra cuddles. To the mamas out there, it's okay to do what is right for your family, not always what the books say.

One night, after Max (age three) had gone to bed, Chloe was sitting outside with Matt and me. It was two months before her fifth birthday. It was a warm summer night, and the three of us were sitting by the fire. Chloe has always been very inquisitive and asks challenging questions daily. We weren't quite ready for her next line of questioning: "Mommy, where is Mimmi, Poppi (her late great grandparents), and Nova (our dog for twelve years)? Where did they go when they died? Can we talk to them? Am I going to be alive for a long time?" She would always talk about ghosts and ask about being able to talk to other people who weren't there. It's almost as if she could feel the missing piece of our family. Maybe knowing about her sister would bring her some peace.

Matt and I shot each other a glance over the flickering fire and knew that it was time to have that dreaded talk with her. "Chloe, can we talk to you about something?" We told her about her sister and about how she was a twin. We did our best to keep it direct and honest. She went through a rainbow of emotions quickly in front of our eyes. First, there was excitement about the idea that she had a sister, then sadness and tears from knowing she wasn't here. We explained how much we miss her and always will. She then looked hopeful that we could talk to her and said that the sky made her think of her sister. She then told us that she knew she had a sister. Whether that was her justifying what was happening or something deeper, we are unsure. Then she shifted to something we didn't expect. She came over and offered comfort and a hug. She was the one consoling *us*. She told me we would always miss her and we would never forget her.

After an array of emotions and questions were done, we stayed up late, hugging, watching the stars, and sitting quietly by the fire. Chloe had fallen asleep in our arms. We carried her to bed and tucked her in as we kissed both her and her brother with a little extra gratitude before heading to sleep ourselves.

Chloe woke up in the middle of the night, as she always does, and asked me to accompany her to the bathroom. We changed the toilet paper to a fresh roll, and she immediately grabbed the cardboard tube and said, "Mom, I need to make something for my sister!" It was 2 am, but how could I say no after the night we had? It was clearly on her mind, and she needed an outlet. She ran to the craft box and pulled out a feather, a couple of pipe cleaners, and a marker. She quickly decorated the tube, added a face, stuck the feather into the pipe cleaners, and brought it back to bed with her.

It was certainly a unique approach to dealing with the news of her sister, but obvious that she wanted something to commemorate her. Early in the morning, Chloe was vigorously explaining to her brother about their sister. He had just turned three and didn't quite feel the news with the same magnitude as Chloe yet, but he is sweet and empathetic. He saw how important it was to her and immediately wanted to do whatever he could to help. The next day, we brought the kids both to Build-A-Bear. Chloe carefully selected a rainbow bear for her sister. We let the kids make all of the choices for the accessories, right down to the "sisters forever" shirt they picked out and the heart, sound, and cotton candy scent.

The bear seemed soothing and helpful. They brought their "Carly Bear" everywhere as if showing her the world around them. The questions continued, of course, and to this day, Chloe refers to her sister daily and always includes her in family counts and discussions. It's amazing how children can play an incredible and important role in processing feelings if we let them shine through. It was the next step for all of us.

Part Ten: Hope

The final part of this chapter is about *hope*. It took some time, but I am so proud to say that I am successfully continuing in my career that I love so much with more inner strength than ever before. That strength comes from knowing that "strong" can also mean emotional and vulnerable when those emotions can be directed in a way that inspires you to go on. I continue to be passionate about helping kids be the best version of themselves through Leadership training at Mastery and helping adults with their health and wellness. My vulnerability allows me to understand and empathize to better understand and help others in their own journeys.

We knew that our family was destined to grow again. It's just something you can feel. Despite the challenges of the journey along the way and the terrifying pain of the past that will always be with us, there is still so much hope, strength, and love to give. While completing this chapter, I am so happy to say I am pregnant once again and **hopeful**. We took our own advice this time and are excitedly sharing the news. We know that our amazing friends and family will be there for us no matter what the future brings. Now that I know the amazing healing power of sharing and leaning on others. I will continue to share my family's story, and I am looking forward to sharing the journey of our new addition later this year!

After trying so many methods to cope, heal and grieve, the part that has been most therapeutic is what I have always been so afraid to do … writing this and sharing the whole truth about our story.

I hope reading this brings you hope: hope that you'll grow stronger through understanding and sharing; hope that your heart will still be able to love as strong even when it is riddled with cracks and scars; and hope that you will find the method that works for you to begin your grieving journey. You don't need to *heal*. You may always have that wound, and even the best superheroes have a painful origin story to look back on.

Conclusion

It has been a privilege and an honor to witness these ten courageous authors go through the process of writing their journey of grief. I love to watch the transformation as the stories progress, as well as the healing or processing of grief that takes place throughout the writing.

Our journey together has been nothing less than amazing. As my authors continue to process their grief, I do as well. What I've learned during the past six years of grieving is that there's always another layer. Will I ever be completely healed? I believe it will be an ongoing process for the rest of my life.

As you read each story, did you notice how different each one is in the path that they took, depending on how their loved one passed? We are all unique in so many ways, so it makes sense that we all grieve differently as well.

As with volume one of *Shining a Light on Grief*, my intention is to help the author continue along their journey of grief as well as be a source of hope and inspiration for the reader. It's healing in so many ways to be able to identify with someone else's story, especially when we feel so alone. Which author did you resonate with the most? What tips did you take away?

I have found that there are so many individuals silently grieving. We never know what someone else is going through as we meet and speak with them. I do my best to give others grace when they are rude, unfriendly, and in a bad mood because we have no idea what's going on in their life. We travel along this journey called life, which can change in an instant.

In the first volume of *Shining a Light on Grief*, I share my story of my son's passing and my journey as I looked at it then. As I continue on this journey, I learn more and more about myself and the grieving process. I love to listen to others talk about their journey because it gives me a different way of looking at things. Recently, I heard that a part of us dies with the person because they are the only ones that remember us in that way. For me, Nathan was my only son, so no one will ever look at me as a mother in that way. While I'm still a mother and those instincts are still there, it can never be the same.

I do believe that our love continues forever, and we will always be connected. It's just in a different way now that he's no longer physical. I believe that death is a transition to who we really are. We're all energy, and energy can never die, only transform.

In compiling these books, I found a true passion that I never knew existed. I'm able to guide these authors along the journey in an understanding and compassionate way. My hope is that this book was helpful to you.

Thank you so much for reading this book.

Watch for more books in the series to be released.

You can find us at www.shiningalightongrief.com.

I'd love to hear about your experience with reading *Shining a Light on Grief.* I can be reached at susan@susanlataille.com.

About Susan Lataille

Susan Lataille has had her own experience with grief after the loss of her son. She knows first hand that grieving is a process that can take you by storm and impact every part of your life. She has found hope and inspiration through others stories and wants you to as well. You can read her story in the first volume of *Shining a Light on Grief.*

Susan Lataille is a Certified Master Grief Coach assisting others along their grief journey through the "Shining a Light on Grief" anthology series, individual and group coaching sessions, workshops, and retreats. She is also a HeartMath® Certified Mentor, Certified International Nutritional Health Coach, Reiki Master, and more.

Email: susan@susanlataille.com
Website: www.shiningalightongrief.com

Made in United States
North Haven, CT
24 December 2023

45689598R00128